## Praise for
### *O for a Thousand Nights to Sleep*

"O for a thousand more books like th̶ ̶ ̶ ̶ ̶ ̶ ̶ ̶ ̶ ̶ ̶ ̶ ̶ ̶ ̶ ̶ ̶ hope
home for new moms with this wit̶ ̶ ̶ ̶ ̶ ̶ ̶ ̶ ̶ ̶ ̶ ̶ ̶ ̶ ̶ ̶ rous
help in every page!"

    —ELISA MORGAN, president a̶̶̶̶

"Lorilee brings humor, grace, and godly wisdom to those early days of parenting. From the fun stuff (the sweet cuddles and coos) to the hard stuff (postpartum depression and sleep deprivation), Lorilee offers the kind of no-nonsense, guilt-free insights new moms crave. Whether you're expecting your first child or your fifth, her great advice and hilarious outlook will have you feeling ready for the challenges of life with a newborn."

    —CARLA BARNHILL, editor of *Christian Parenting Today*
      and mother of two

"Lorilee Craker is the fresh new voice for mothers everywhere! Her exacting wit, engaging prose, encouraging words, and sanity-saving tips are as precious and life altering as a newborn baby. I have two hopes: First, that every new mother holds her baby in one arm and this book in the other, and second, that Lorilee keeps writing more books. She is an excellent writer with a warm, funny, conversational style. I highly recommend *O for a Thousand Nights to Sleep* and Lorilee's sage advice!"

    —DEBRA WATERHOUSE, M.P.H., R.D., author of *Outsmarting the*
      *Female Fat Cell—After Pregnancy*

"I love this book! What a great insight into all the things that come with having a baby: frustration, wonder, and humor. I especially love the perspective on friends and family and all the unwanted advice. This book is hilarious, truthful, and informative."

    —CINDY MORGAN, singer and songwriter

"Almost as much as they need a good night's sleep, new moms need a good laugh. In *O for a Thousand Nights to Sleep*, Craker combines solid advice with laugh-out-loud descriptions of typical first-year dilemmas. The voices of other moms, woven into each chapter, reassure us that there are many ways to do this mommy thing well. And above all, Craker encourages readers to depend on faith in God to get through the toughest moments with joy to spare."

    —DEBRA RIENSTRA, author of *Great with Child*

"Every mother will identify with Lorilee Craker's humorous, honest, and down-to-earth look at what it takes to survive baby's first year. From the agony of colic to the ecstasy of that first step, *O for a Thousand Nights to Sleep* maps the course through the terrain of new parenthood. Lorilee's prose is filled with wonder, discovery, and the joy that abounds as we are given the gift to see the miracle of life anew in our baby's eyes. I highly recommend it!"

    —TRACI DEPREE, author of *A Can of Peas* and mother of four

"You've heard of soccer moms? Well, Lorilee Craker is a hockey mom. She's a hockey fan of the first order, and she has written some bang-up articles about hockey players. She brings hockey-type energy to everything she writes, even if it's about something ten times harder than playing hockey—being a mom. She always pulls off the writer's hat trick (clever, clear, and insightful), and this book is no exception."

    —DAVE BRANON, managing editor of *Sports Spectrum* magazine
       and author of more than a dozen books

"I laughed, I cried! I love how this book gives so many different perspectives and covers so many topics. This is lighthearted yet serious coaching for the sport of baby rearing! 'I'm ready, Coach! Put me in!' "

    —SHANNON DUNN-DOWNING, U.S. Olympian and new mom

# O for a Thousand Nights to Sleep

## An Eye-Opening Guide to the Wonder-Filled Months of Baby's First Year

■ ■ ■

## LORILEE CRAKER

WATERBROOK
PRESS

O FOR A THOUSAND NIGHTS TO SLEEP
PUBLISHED BY WATERBROOK PRESS
2375 Telstar Drive, Suite 160
Colorado Springs, Colorado 80920
*A division of Random House, Inc.*

The author of this book is not a physician, and the ideas, procedures, and suggestions in this book are not intended as a substitute for the medical advice of a trained health professional. All matters regarding your health and your baby's health require medical supervision. Consult your physician before adopting the suggestions in this book, as well as about any condition that may require diagnosis or medical attention. The author and publisher disclaim any liability arising directly or indirectly from the use of the book.

All Scripture quotations, unless otherwise indicated, are taken from the *Holy Bible, New International Version*®. NIV®. Copyright © 1973, 1978, 1984 by International Bible Society. Used by permission of Zondervan Publishing House. All rights reserved.

ISBN 1-57856-487-5

Copyright © 2003 by Lorilee Craker

Library of Congress Cataloging-in-Publication Data
Craker, Lorilee.
    O for a thousand nights to sleep : an eye-opening guide to the wonder-filled months of baby's first year / Lorilee Craker.
        p. cm.
    ISBN 1-57856-487-5
    1. Infants—Care—Popular works.  I. Title: Guide to the wonder-filled months of baby's first year. II. Title.
    RJ61 .C885 2003
    649'.122—dc21

                                                                    2002152720

Printed in the United States of America
2003—First Edition

10 9 8 7 6 5 4 3 2 1

With love and thanksgiving for Allan Loewen,
a "don't call me Uncle" uncle, treasured confidant,
and kindred spirit, now and always.

Fight the good fight, Uncle Al,
and whatever happens,
someday I'll see you on the other side.

# Contents

*Month Seven:*

*You and Your New Body • Ditch the Stress of Dieting • Baby Sign Language • On the Relationship Seat: Workout Buddies • Care for Tiny Teeth • Great Giggles • Brain-Boosting Toys for 6- to 9-Month-Olds • The Top Ten Ways to Make a Baby Laugh*

*Month Eight:*

*Express Those Feelings, Baby! • Magnificent Money Savers • The Top Ten Ways to Save a Buck • Every Parent Worries • On the Relationship Seat: The Prince of Peace • Bonus Top Ten: Things You Could Worry About but Probably Shouldn't! • You Hold the Baby; Let Jesus Hold You*

*Month Nine:*

*The Nine-Month "Touchpoint" • Travel Tips • Baby-Keen Eyesight • Eating out with Baby • Things to Take on Any Outing • On the Relationship Seat: Long-Distance Grandparents*

*Month Ten:*

*The Babbling Baby • Babyproofing Whats and What-Nots • Directing Baby Gently Toward Good (and Safe!) Behavior • On the Relationship Seat: Of In-Laws and Outlaws • Babyhood Gross-Outs • The Top Ten Safety Measures to Take at Home*

# Acknowledgments

Many, many thanks to the gracious and wonderful people in my life who have, in some way, accelerated the writing of this book:

- Kinfolk: My parents, Abe and Linda Reimer, for their love, prayers, and encouragement. Under the same category, my gratitude to Ken and Linda Craker, Dan and Tina Reimer, Lorraine and Tracy Bush, and Mike and Jodi Connell.

- As always, appreciation to George and Pat Vanderlaan, for proving over and over that the definition of family happily includes non-relatives.

- To my friends, who enrich my life and make me laugh: Bonnie Anderson, Carla Klassen, Nancy Rubin, Lisa Freire, Becky Wertz Walker, Stephanie Nelson, Rachel Vanderlaan, Debbie Scott, and Mary Jo Haab.

- Sheri Rodriguez, Juliana Clink, and Joanne Swart, for being "soul sisters" and for discipling me by the way they live their lives. And all the ladies who attend "Women Growing in Grace" at Madison Square Church.

- Fellow writers Christine Scott, Kathleen Morgan, and Ann Byle, for encouragement and inspiration.

- Dr. Akourkour Addy, for nurturing this new mom and being the kind of doctor my kids can't wait to see!

- The bookies at WaterBrook Press: Don Pape, Laura Barker, Ginia Hairston, Laura Wright, et al., for your enthusiasm and support, and the best Canadian distributors, like, ever: Bob Wood and Pat Chown, for going the extra kilometer for me and my books!

Same song, different verse…

- For abiding encouragement and advice, my thanks to Twila Bennett (Go Amy!) and Dwight Baker, even though he steals my husband for fishing trips.
- Special thanks to Erin Healy, for being unflappable and encouraging, a dream editor, and an unexpected blessing.
- As always, I am indebted to Lisa Tawn Bergren for believing in me. I want to be like you when I grow up.

And bountiful love, kisses, and hugs to my three men: Doyle (love ya, Buck!), Jonah, and Ezra. My cup overflows!

# Introduction

I'm a baby junkie. There. I said it. The world is divided, loosely, between "baby people" and "kid people," and then there are a few who don't much care for either. Don't get me wrong. Children can be very lovable and endearing and cute. I love my two tots dearly. But there's something about a baby that makes me melt like butter.

Their newness—as Dickens said, babies are "fresh from God"—their helplessness, and their miniscule proportions all converge to make this irresistible, powdery-smelling package that's impossible to beat. Footie pajamas, silky, teeny wisps of hair, toes like Niblets—I could go on. *Butter.*

Lest you're going into sugar shock from my sappy ramblings, let me tell you that I do know babies have a dark side, especially when it's you they call upon for care and feeding. For starters, there are the diaper detonations that occur at the least timely moments, the weirdness of being milked like a cow, and that teeth-gnashing, head-splitting standby: screaming.

I remember holding my first baby, Jonah, as he yelled his brains out for three hours one night and thinking that I was about to lose it—if not consciousness, then sanity. He provided quite the crash course in Babyhood 101, that kid of mine. Not only did he have a case of colic, but he also was what is known as an "Urper." You'll know what I'm talking about if your munchkin likes to disgorge breakfast, lunch, and dinner on the floor, himself, you, the cat, and so forth. Baby number two wasn't a screamer (praise Yahweh!), and he kept most of his meals to himself. But Ezra had new tricks up his sleeve, such as not sleeping through the night for nine months of his life.

This book attempts to present a rounded picture of Baby's first year, covering the thrill of bonding and bathing as well as the agony of engorged breasts and sleep deprivation. I wanted you, the new mama, to benefit from my numerous mistakes and lessons learned. Like pregnancy, your baby's first year of life is an intense time. I also wanted to try to help you lighten up here and there. Because when you realize you've got poop under your fingernails (or when you find yourself in any of the other ludicrous situations that will present themselves this year), you can choose to either fling yourself on the ground and scream into the carpet, or laugh until pop comes out your nose.

The poignant, beautiful moments of your baby's first year are special and sacred. You may be tempted to zoom in on your precious progeny while everyone else—your family, your buddies, even your husband—fades to black. This book will help you get a better grip on your new role while keeping strong connections with your husband, your family and friends, and your heavenly Father. When you have a sense of balance in your key relationships, your role as a mom will be more fun and rewarding.

I hope and pray—really—that these stories, tips, lists, and letters will smooth your journey into motherhood. Most of all, though, hold on to this amazing, precious year of your life. When you gaze at your sleeping bundle, cradled in your arms, you'll realize as never before how much God must love you—and your baby—to have given the world His.

# Welcome to Dairy Queen! May I Take Your Order?

This is it, the moment you have been both dreading and anticipating for months now: It's time for you to feed your baby via your own two mammaries, for Pete's sake! They—"The Girls," that is—previously operated strictly as ornamental fixtures, amusement centers, and possibly jogging hindrances. But now they have been promoted to a different department and given a completely new and serious function.

The lactation consultants you bid a fond farewell to at the hospital are only a phone call away, true, but you really, truly, madly, deeply want to do this on your own and, hopefully, with a modicum of accuracy.

The pillows are wedged under your arms, and nutritious snacks are assembled on the nearby "nursing station," where the remote control and a glass of milk also stand at the ready.

You've repositioned the baby several times—in the cradle, the cross-cradle, and the clutch, to name three—and you and she have opted for one that feels pretty good to both of you. You look down at her; she looks up at you, her itty-bitty mouth making that little *O* shape. Show time.

"Welcome to Dairy Queen! May I take your order?" you say, hoping to lighten the mood a little. Yup, you're feeling kind of bovine. Why? Because you're being milked. Milked! It's altogether bizarre, yet here you are, squirting streams of an actual dairylike product, not into a galvanized bucket but into your baby's mouth.

Or at least this is the hoped-for result.

What should be the most natural thing in the world can be distinctly unnatural, not to mention awkward, painful, and inconvenient. But it's so utterly beneficial for Baby, and your friends have told you that the bonding nursing provides is phenomenal, so you're giving it a try. Good for you! And I mean that: Breast-feeding is something to be proud of.

## The Combo Mambo

To breast-feed or bottle-feed? In most cases it doesn't have to be all or nothing. A growing number of moms are choosing to feed their babies a combination of breast milk and formula. When I had Jonah, I worried that he wasn't getting enough milk, so I started giving him a bottle a day, usually right before he fell asleep for the "night" (three or four hours for the first few weeks). Breast milk is easily digested, and Jonah was always hungry again two hours after I nursed. Formula seemed to stick to his ribs better, which meant I could snooze a little while longer—precious! Even better, my husband, Doyle, could heave himself out of bed once in a while and cover night duty completely—priceless.

By the time Ezra came along, I'd already planned to combo feed him even though I knew by that time that babies get enough chow from nursing (only 5 percent of women have a bona fide insufficient milk supply). My motive was to get sleep, and more of it, so Baby Ez got a bottle for a midnight snack from day three on. Nipple confusion was never an issue for anyone but me, since I couldn't remember which of the Girls was hit on last.

Maria Pruis (my lactation consultant) advises new moms to hold off on supplementing until six weeks, when a woman's milk supply is regulated. In hindsight, I wish I could have held off until then, because in fact I did mess up my milk supply, a little, anyway. Personally, I found it harder to nurse exclusively with Ez simply because I had to care for his big bro as well. It seemed that every time we were about to go somewhere—church, a friend's house, the mall—it was lunchtime for Ez, and we just didn't have forty minutes to spare to sit down and breast-feed. Experts say, and my experience bears this out, that supplementing with one bottle can lead to two, then three a day, and eventually a shrinking milk supply.

*Baby Talk* magazine did their readers an incredible service with an enlightening survey of how moms feed and how they feel about it—really feel about it. Among the findings:

- Breast-feeding moms think formula-feeding moms are short-changing their babies...but bottle-feeders don't feel criticized and basically don't care if they are.
- Formula gals are supportive and even a little jealous of their nursing friends...but overall are happy with their choice.

Here's where the story got real interesting for me and the estimated one-third of new moms who do the combo:

- 74 percent of combo moms surveyed said they have "the best of both worlds."

 **Bottle Love**

Nursing is not for everyone, and I refuse to make the many bottle-feeders out there feel guilty. Yes, "breast is best," as we all know, but babies who are fed with love from a bottle thrive too. Most of you reading this book right now weren't breast-fed simply because it wasn't really thought of as the best way to go back in the days when our moms had us. Look how we turned out! The Mammary Militia out there means well, I'm pretty sure, but don't let any of the inflammatory rhetoric get to you. Babies need love above all, even more than they need breast milk! So hold your baby close when you give him his bottle and feel good about the great job you are doing nurturing and caring for him!

- 50 percent admitted to being disappointed that they couldn't breast-feed exclusively.
- 70 percent say they have not been slammed for their feeding choice by a fellow mom. "But the ones who have been are more upset than any other group of moms. Unlike the full-time formula feeders, who 'didn't care' when someone gave them a hard time, the combo moms were angered (74 percent), frustrated (72 percent), and hurt (63 percent) by their critics."[1]

Overall, though, this group was "thrilled" by the way their choice worked out, and—with a couple of caveats—so was I. My boys got the health bennies of breast milk, yet their dad and grandparents were able to share in occasional feedings—great for bonding! During those first few weeks, which seem like one big nursing marathon, I got a few key mental health breaks here and there, and Doyle and I were even able to indulge in some couple time. Next time—if there is a next time—I'll attempt to be more discretionary in my use of bottles, knowing what I know now about milk supply. Would I be a combo mom again? Definitely.

## Keeping Friends

Nobody likes a strident, holier-than-thou breast-feeder, no matter how fantastic the method is for humankind. Seriously, don't get smug about nursing; your friends will thank you. Bottle-feeding is not child abuse. The choice to feed by breast or bottle is not a moral or spiritual issue. This is definitely one of those live-and-let-live kinds of things, which means we all need to support each other and try to remember the old maxim "You don't really know a woman until you've felt the pain of her mastitis."

Sheri lost a friendship over nursing, if you can believe it. When Sheri's son Jacob was born, an old pal designated herself "Lactation Cheerleader" and gave the new mom books on breast-feeding as a baby gift. Of course, the newly milk-producing need all the encouragement they can get, so this support system was great—until the friend got testy when Sheri quit after a few weeks. "She just didn't try hard enough," she once hissed to another friend loudly enough for Sheri to hear. In truth, Sheri *had* tried, employing the assistance of no fewer than five lactation consultants in her home the first week. When the woman smugly told Sheri she would be missing "the most special aspect of being a mom" by not breast-feeding, well, their friendship hit the skids and has never recovered.

I had a similar experience once when telling a friend about my plans to combo-feed my second child. Explaining how one bottle in the night did wonders for my sleeping life made no impression on this woman. She came at the issue from every which way, trying to persuade me that even one feeding from a "cold, plastic bottle" per twenty-four-hour period was wrong, dead wrong. I finally had to explain that yes, sleep was more important to me than exclusive nursing because, frankly, I had a mild case of MS, and fatigue could trigger a flareup. She didn't even bat an eyelash over this news and continued to badger me as though I were forcing my baby to drink dog shampoo or something.

Lisa chose to bottle-feed baby number three, Margaret, after having combo-fed Alexandra and Emma. Why? During her pregnancy, Lisa began to battle depression, and she expected to get hit hard with post-partum depression after her delivery. She decided that the best choice for her and her family would be to immediately begin a course of antidepressants. "I wanted to be able to take care of my baby properly, and I knew this was the best way," she says. Not everyone agreed with her. Nurses in the hospital pestered her with questions about why she wasn't nursing, and when she finally told them why, they pushed her to find an antidepressant that would be safe to take while nursing. "They probably meant well, but I felt really pushed. This was my own private choice. I didn't want to mess around with trying different meds; I wanted the one I already knew worked with my body."

Lisa adds that, after all the turmoil of having her decision questioned, her bottle-fed child experienced fewer colds and ear infections than her breast-fed older sisters. (Usually the reverse is true. Statistically speaking,

 **The Best Nursing Advice I Ever Got**

"My beloved friend Aviva is a model mother and had three children before I had mine. When I called her in tears, she said, 'Give it a full six weeks. Keep trying. Don't get frustrated. You can't know for sure if it's not for you until you've tried for six weeks. Nursing is not the warm, wonderful, relaxing, bonding experience that ads make it out to be. It's hard work, it hurts sometimes, and you have to give it a fair chance. Both you and the baby are learning, but when you finally get it, you'll be glad you kept trying because it's very rewarding.' I started counting the days until I could finally throw in the towel, but by the time six weeks had gone by, Amelia and I were like old pros."

—Laura

"Some wise woman (bless whoever she is) told me to make middle-of-the-night feedings as boring for the baby as possible. I always went to my daughter when she cried and fed her every three to four hours through the night, but I kept the lights off, fed her in a rocker close to her crib, and didn't spend time talking, singing, or having much stimulating eye contact with her during the wee hours. She always went back to sleep easily after these feedings and, in fact, started sleeping through the night at exactly eight weeks."

—Michelle

"Get support, whether it be other breast-feeding moms or a more formal support group. For me, with each baby I knew more breast-feeders and thus had more encouragement, so I stuck with it longer.

breast-fed babies typically emerge with more robust health. Still, there are a myriad reasons why some babies get ear infections and colds, and some cruise through babyhood as healthy as horses. Nursing is just one factor.)

Another biggie: *breast pads.* I'm sure every mom has her leaking story, but the first time I went to church with my first baby, I knew he was getting hungry—the whole emotions thing, you know. I started leaking like crazy. Friends wanted to hold him, and I couldn't let them or they would see my nice wet shirt! Thank goodness for lots of blankets! Buy breast pads before the baby is born. I had *no* idea I even needed them. Of course I ended up sending my husband to the store when the baby was a few days old, and well, men are men, if you know what I mean!"

—Amy

"Rub Vitamin E capsules on your nipples after every feeding. My sister-in-law told me this tip and I can't believe how well it's prevented dryness, cracking, and soreness!"

—Mary Jo

"The hardest thing for me about breast-feeding was the initial pain associated with the baby latching on. This lasted the first two weeks or so with each of my girls. It was so bad I literally had to dig my toes into the carpet. After the first couple of weeks, though, I had no problem. The best pieces of advice I got were to relax, drink a glass of water while you nurse, totally soak up the bonding time nursing provides, and don't let nursing hold you back from going places (work it into your normal routines)."

—Deone

Breast-feeding is wonderful, extremely nutritious, money-saving, and so on, but it's not worth hurting someone or losing a friendship.

## "Say 'Awww'"

One of the great challenges of nursing is getting a narcoleptic little nub to open his mouth wide enough to latch on correctly. Maria, my wonderful lactation consultant, gave me a great tip when I was in the first days of nursing Ezra. "Play the open mouth game," she suggested. "Open your mouth as wide as you can, and Baby will imitate you." *Imitate me? Isn't he a bit young to be asked to perform a mimic routine?* I wondered. Actually, this method worked—some of the time anyway. See, babies need to figure out that din-din will not be served until their mouths are as Grand Canyon–like as they can manage. As you probably have heard by now, Baby has to grab on to not just your nipple but also the areola surrounding it for any decent sucking action. "Hey, I wanna see molars back there!" might be a good way to start the pep talk.

Here's a fascinating tidbit from Janet Tamaro's book, *So That's What They're For:* "Once your areola and nipple are in your baby's mouth, your nipple will be pulled out about three times its normal resting length. Don't worry. It was made to stretch. That's because the baby needs to form the areola tissue into a teat."[2] Teat, huh? That's pretty bovine terminology, but hey, that's what they are.

(By the way, if you are curious as to what your nipple looks like extended to three times its normal length, just use one of those handheld plastic pumps. The first time you do this, the visual will give you and your whole family a slightly *Ripley's Believe It or Not* experience. Dawn was pumping in her bedroom one day when her son Reuben burst into the room. Wide-eyed with amazement, Reuben exclaimed, "Mommy, you have a penis!" Dawn and her husband are socking money away for that biggie therapy bill!)

**Voices**

"I've flunked breast-feeding. I never could make enough milk. I've drunk enough water to sink a ship. I've pumped until my boobs hurt. I've taken fenugreek and Reglan, and I've drunk Mother's Milk Tea. I'm exhausted. Obviously my baby gets nutrition from that stupid formula, and that seems to fill up his tummy, so I throw in the towel."

—Barb

"I never had trouble getting my baby to latch on. But getting her to let go was a different story. (And not because she wasn't getting enough. I have photos to prove it: she was in the ninety-ninth percentile for weight!) She turned my breasts into slingshots regularly until Mom suggested I use my pinkie finger to the break suction at the corner of her mouth before pulling her off. What a relief!"

—Christy

"When Tatum was very small, we had an awful time nursing. For the first three days of her life, she just refused to latch on. Even after that, at times she just wouldn't suck. It also took us a long time to learn to nurse lying down. At night, I hated to turn on the light because then it would wake me up completely, so I used to feel my way around her face to help her latch on. One night, we were lying in bed, and I was doing my utmost to latch her on. And she just wouldn't nurse. I kept trying and trying. Finally in frustration I turned on the light. Then I noticed that Tatum had turned her head—and I had spent the last ten minutes shoving my nipple into her ear!"

—Kelly

# What to Eat When You're Expecting
# (Milk to Come Out of Your Being)

If you're dying for a shot of java to get you going on those oh-so-bleary mornings, I have good news: Go for it! Seriously, I got this info straight from the horse's mouth, the horse being, of course, La Leche League. Now, we all know these ladies are not exactly wishy-washy when it comes to the topic of breast-feeding, so I almost fell out of my chair when I heard that nursing moms can have up to five cups of joe a day!

I have no idea why, but magazines, other moms, and even doctors will tell you to lay off coffee because it gets into the breast milk and causes Baby to be cranky. But here's the straight story, in black and white: "According to LLL's *The Breast-feeding Answer Book,* moderate intake of caffeine (the amount in five or fewer 5-ounce cups of coffee per day, or less than 750 ml per day) causes no problems for most breast-feeding mothers and babies."[3]

Still not convinced? Here's more:

"Caffeine ingestion has been singled out for discussion because it is a frequent concern, but the data provided in most reviews are misleading. With a given dose of caffeine that is comparable to that in a cup of coffee, the level in the milk is low (1 percent of level in mother), and the level in the infant's plasma is also low."[4]

While it's true that what goes into your body usually does make its way into your milk supply, the amount is generally a tiny fraction of what you ingest—about 1 percent, as we just learned. So it really doesn't do any good to bravely pass on the chocolate chip scones at your baby shower. The amount of caffeine getting through wouldn't be enough to give a flea the jitters, never mind your strapping seven pounder.

They say cauliflower is one of the worst perpetrators of gassiness in your baby, so if you are a huge cauliflower enthusiast, by all means LAY OFF for a while and see if Gassy Gus lets up on the toots. (I mean, is that so hard? Cauliflower?)

##  Of Cabbages and Things

- Wear a supportive nursing bra even during the night. Be sure it isn't too tight.
- Nurse every two to three hours. Make sure your baby has a go on both breasts—ten to twenty minutes each—at each feeding and is swallowing well and softening the breast after each nursing.
- Don't let Baby latch on and suckle when the areola—the dark area around your nipple—is very firm. Why? Two words: nipple damage. Yee-ooooww! To help your baby latch on, manually express milk until the areola softens. It may be easier to manually express milk in the shower; the warm water may cause enough leakage to soften the areola. Note: Your baby may have a harder time latching on when your breasts are engorged. Be patient and keep trying!
- While your baby nurses, gently massage the breast he's on. This encourages milk to flow and will help relieve some of the tightness and discomfort.
- To soothe the pain and help relieve swelling, apply cold packs to the breast for a short period after nursing. Crushed ice in a plastic bag works well.
- Some women find relief by applying fresh green cabbage leaves to their breasts. I'm not sure why this works, but it apparently does, so stock up on cabbage!
- If you're really in pain, take acetaminophen (like Tylenol) or a mild pain reliever prescribed by your healthcare provider.
- Don't apply direct heat, such as warm washcloths, heating pads, or hot water bottles, to your engorged breasts unless it's to soften the areola and help your milk let down. Rather than alleviate the pain, this may aggravate the condition.

The list of possible foods that could infiltrate your milk and result in tummy commotion is endless: cabbage, onion, garlic, broccoli, Brussels sprouts, peppers, cucumbers, and turnips. Cow's milk products (such as milk, cheese, yogurt, and even butter) in your diet are said to possibly induce gas or an allergic reaction in your baby. Citrus fruit such as oranges, lemons, limes, grapefruit, and tangerines may cause hives. Eggs, wheat, corn, fish, peanuts, nuts, and soy are touted as irritants too. So basically, what these people would have us believe is that we can't eat much. Maybe ground beef and apples, but that's about it.

If you or your main man are allergic to ground beef and apples, let's say, or any other food substance, steer clear for about ten days and see if Baby's moods lighten up a little. Basically, food allergies are rare in breast-fed babies because breast milk coats their intestines, making it unlikely an unlovable food bit gets through.

     **Stat Flash**

According to Ross Laboratory's Feeding Survey in 1995, 60 percent of women were breast-feeding at hospital discharge, and 21 percent were breast-feeding at six months of age. These rates vary markedly depending on maternal age, ethnic group, family income, and maternal education.[5]

One thing is definite: No matter what you eat, you are going to be ravenous, a predator on the prowl for those five hundred extra calories you need to gobble down. Just make sure you don't add a digit to the five hundred and make it five thousand extra calories, because then your thighs are just plain in trouble. (On second thought, it's still early. Eat what you like, and we'll save our little weight loss discussion for another day.)

WARNING: Known milk boosters such as ground fenugreek, anise, borage, raspberry leaves, blessed thistle, saw palmetto, dill, chaste tree, garlic, nettles, fennel seeds, goat's rue, false unicorn root, vervain, and cinnamon taken in high doses can make you smell like a pancake. Apparently these herbs, which are found in Mother's Milk Tea, infuse your sweat with an eau de maple syrup fragrance. So if you don't want loved ones sniffing you and feeling suddenly inspired to whip up a batch of Belgian waffles, consider yourself forewarned.

## "Hey You, Lady with the Blanket over Your Head!"

Breast-feeding in public is something I never got the hang of. Not that I have a problem with women who nurse their babies at the mall, the airport, church—wherever. To be honest, I envy them.

My husband, Doyle, and I recently attended our first parent-teacher conference at the preschool Jonah goes to. Waiting in the hall outside the classroom was another couple we knew slightly. They had just had their third baby, and the newborn was snoozing contentedly in his mother's arms—or at least that's what he appeared to be doing. Doyle leaned over for a closer look at the baby's face, and—uh oh!—got a look at more than he ever bargained for. My well-meaning husband withdrew from the scene rather quickly, retreating to the janitor's closet in hopes that the earth would swallow him up. He felt like an idiot, a pervert, and a doofus all in the same fell swoop. Now I have to come up with a way to say, "Hey, sorry that my husband accidentally saw a sliver of your breast."

### Quotable

"Babies don't realize or care that they are on the bus or in the bookstore and not in Breast Milk Bistro or on their couch at home."[6]
—Gwen Zepeda

All that to say, these things can and will happen. Both my babes are Christmas munchkins, so twice I found myself in the midst of crash-course nursing in the thick of swarming relatives. The men looked away, anyplace but at me, and the women surreptitiously glanced at me to see if I needed help or a tip or two. One time I kept trying to get Jonah to latch on, while still maintaining decency, and it just wasn't working. Finally I gave up and covered both Jonah and myself with a blanket, creating a tent that was both private and unbearably stuffy. It's a tough call whether I looked sillier as a ghost with no eyeholes or, later, as a gasping diver coming up for air with sweaty bangs matted to my forehead. But at least the kid got his brunch, which is the main thing, right?

I found it much more relaxing—and cooler—to just retreat to a private space somewhere and hang with the baby for forty minutes or so. Some of my friends love nursing tops, tailored to allow nursing with a minimum of flesh showing. Draping a diaper or receiving blanket over the baby cuts down on the flash factor too. At the mall, scout out a lounge area by the bathroom, where you can feed in private.

Your husband or a friend can help by standing in front of you or holding a blanket up while you get situated, at least during the first few weeks, when you may want to see what it is you're doing. If you're really committed, invest in a nursing blanket, a more sophisticated cover-up that will allow you to see the baby without exposing you or constantly slipping off.

If all else fails, and it very well might, just whip out a breast and do what you have to do. It's legal, and chances are you'll never see these people again (well, we hope).

## Pump at Work: a Win-Win

When it's time to return to the office, you don't necessarily have to give up nursing. In fact, many women continue breast-feeding by pumping at work. It's not always easy, but you can keep the uber-nutrition of breast milk in your baby's body and feel more connected with him while away. Best of all, you get to come home to a baby who wants you to feed and snuggle with him! Here's a list of do's for successful pumping:

## Have Others Hold Off Feeding

Ask Daddy, Grandma, Nanny Fran, or whoever your caregiver happens to be to hold off on feeding your little one for an hour or so before you come home, or to just give her enough to tide her over until the Dairy Queen arrives.

## Assemble a Supply

Start assembling a supply of pumped and frozen breast milk before you return to work. You'll feel more confident about the process after you've been through it a few times.

## Avoid Leaks

You'll need bottles, access to a refrigerator, a pump (double electric works best), and breast pads to prevent those oh-so-mortifying leaks! Keep a cooler in the car for the ride home so all your efforts won't spoil before you get to Baby.

## Find a Good Place to Pump

Most pumping personnel unfortunately have to make do with the bathroom stall, but check around for empty offices and conference rooms.

 **Li'l Biters**

When Baby cuts her first tooth, she may start using your nipples as a teething ring (more yee-ooooww!). If you rub her gums with your finger before she starts feeding, that in itself may prevent biting. She can't suck and bite at the same time, so try and watch for her to come unlatched. If she's chewing, experts say she may be done chowing, too. Say "no biting" in a manner that suggests you ain't kidding, or employ a gentle flick to her cheek next time she bites. Sounds harsh, but she'll get the picture soon enough.

### Relax

Try to take some deep breaths and relax. Sipping on a cool drink might help too. Some breast-feeders have found that looking at Baby's photo or inhaling a whiff of his baby-scented pajamas helps trigger milk letdown.

### Stick to a Schedule

Pump at the same time every day, twice a day, if you can.

### Label Your Milk

Label your breast milk clearly so your coworkers don't accidentally take a sip. (It sounds preposterous, but we've all heard stories...)

### Thaw; Don't Nuke

Thaw the milk in a saucepan or bowl of warm water. Apparently nuking breast milk can destroy some nutrients.

## You and Old Faithful Have Something in Common

There's leaking, and then there's leaking, if you know what I mean. Some women experience the slightest little trickles, once in a great while, and always at home in their pajamas. Then there are those of us who have gushed geysers of liquid, our errant breasts acting like a fire hydrant gone berserk in the most inopportune of places, while we are wearing the least practical and most showcasing type of outfits known to womankind. Why? Because we simply didn't believe it could happen to us. No matter what they say about breast pads and pumping, and despite leaking horror stories told behind closed doors (and over lunch, in the elevator, and at the mall), you didn't buy it, did you? Sad to say, neither did I, as the choir at my church knows full well.

Beckie, a second-time mom, experienced a virtual deluge of milk so great one evening that she had to excuse herself from the dinner table. Yes, it happened at dinner, where there were guests. *Guests.* As in nonimmediate-family-members. When she got up from the table, Beckie had to bend over a towel to catch the milk that had soaked through two layers of clothing and was threatening to drip into the food.

You may never leak milk, or like Beckie, you may spew forth like Old Faithful. Leaking or spraying breasts are a normal, though a sometimes gee-was-my-face-red part of breast-feeding. Mornings, when your milk supply is most bountiful, tend to be leaky times for many women throughout nursing. Your breasts may also dribble when they become so full of milk that they overflow or when your letdown kicks in unexpectedly (for instance, when another baby in the room starts to cry).

In a cruel twist of fate, some of us discover that leaking and engorgement are inextricably linked. Engorgement is one of the strangest aspects of nursing, that those once B-cup breasts will inflate to at least one cup size bigger, not counting how massive they are when engorged. Six weeks after Jonah was born, my husband was a groomsman in his cousin's wedding. I didn't figure I'd be able to nurse at the wedding, since I could barely preserve modesty while breast-feeding in public with a sweatshirt on, never mind a dress. So with great angst (see Month 11), we left our new baby in the capable hands of his grandparents and ventured out to our first social occasion alone since our son's birth. It was a disaster of epic proportions.

About an hour into the wedding, I could feel that telltale tingle, alerting me to the distinct possibility of a letdown in the next few moments. But I didn't worry, since I—savvy me—had brought along breast pads. Breast pads, schmeastpads! Those wimpy cotton puffs were drenched in no time. Of course had I thought to bring more than one pair, the situation may well have been salvaged. So I sprint-hobbled to the bathroom, where I gaped with horror at the two concrete bowling balls now attached to my chest. *Well,* you might be saying to yourself, *that's not the end of the world. Just pump and those monolithic mams will shrink back in no time.* Well, "savvy me" had failed to bring her hand pump! What a dopey thing to do, but as they say, hindsight is 20/20. The moral of the story is, don't spend the reception of a swanky wedding wishing for a go at the buffet table but trapped in a bathroom stall, hand-expressing milk into the toilet and stifling bellows of pain! Instead, prepare for engorgement, I beg you! Bring either your baby or a pump with you everywhere you go, stockpile breast pads, and keep an extra top in your purse, car, or diaper bag.

There's no quick fix for leaking, although a few precautionary measures are prudent. Nurse often and try out different positions. If you feel a letdown at an untimely moment, cross your arms and hug yourself. This may stop the leak in its tracks, and it may camouflage the huge wet stain on your shirt. Or, if a Worst Case Scenario develops, and your boss/lab partner/the UPS man/the president is standing on your doorstep, staring at you in vast discomfort while Lake Erie develops on your chest, well, it's all over. You've just got to hold your head high, and thank him graciously for the project/homework/package/Congressional Medal of Honor, shut the door, and try to move on with your life. By your baby's tenth week, your cups should no longer be running over.

Dear Ezra,

I think Daddy and I are finally over the shock of you being a boy! As I tell everyone, I wouldn't trade you for a whole bunch of girls. You are absolutely precious. Just as I had hoped, you have a calm spirit and, so far, no signs of the Big C: colic! I remember pacing the floors with your brother at all hours, praying he would stop yelling. In light of that memory, we feel so grateful that you are not a screamer. Actually, you pretty much sleep all the time. In fact, it's hard to get you to wake up for your feedings. When I look down at you, sucking away so vigorously, my heart just wells up with so much emotion. I think you are enormously handsome, with your broad nose and your dark blue eyes and your perfect, chubby cheeks. And I know already you are going to be Mama's snuggler. When you lie on my chest, you always nestle your face into my neck. I am so glad you're my cuddle-bug! I can't help myself from covering your face with kisses. Daddy says he can't get the glitter from my lip gloss off your face, even with soap and water! So you are "very sparkly," in the words of the Rainman. I wonder what these early traits—serene, affectionate—mean for your future as a boy and a man?

Opa and Oma were here for Christmas, and they were immediately as taken with you as they were with Jonah. Opa spent lots of time holding you as you slept, and he protested vigorously when we told him to wake you up from time to time! You love to be wrapped tightly, and you dislike being cold. (Opa says, "Smart guy!") The bath is not your favorite place, as you strenuously attested last time we gave you a good dunking.

When I took you for your two-week appointment, Dr. Addy weighed you, and you had already gained a pound plus beyond your birthweight. She also tested all your reflexes, and when she tried out your "walking" reflex (she held you up and you "walked" on your chubby little legs), she said it was one of the best she had ever seen! So maybe you will be athletic, like Jonah and your daddy. Whatever and whomever you become, we treasure this, the beginning of your life. I adore you.

Love,

Mommy

—Lorilee Craker, mother of Jonah and Ezra

# Great Beginnings, Great-Aunt Ethel, and Great Balls of Fire! You're Someone's Ma!

*Milemarker!* "By about four weeks, new babies have learned special behavioral patterns for each parent. For a mother, the baby's extremities, movements, and facial behaviors are smooth and low key in anticipation of their low-keyed, rhythmic interaction. With the father, the baby's facial features all go up, the extremities tense and waiting, as if the new baby had already learned that his father played with him."[1]

## Fascinating!

Isn't it amazing how much you can adore a person who just developed a bowel movement all over you? That this jerky, gnomish-looking sprite with curled fists and puffy eyes could make your heart stop? Go figure. But don't worry, New Mama, there's plenty more where that came from, both love seizures and diaper explosions.

Despite the fact that Baby Brutus has about eight naps a day, you're probably finding it hard to get anything accomplished. In fact, I imagine you're still in your pj's, you haven't taken a shower, and—wait a sec—did you brush your teeth? Don't worry if your hygiene has taken a hit. Right now you're in survival mode, and you know how gnarly our television friends from *Survivor* got—without even a baby to show for their grungi-ness—even in the first week.

Hopefully Great-aunt Ethel will find your Snoopy sleep-shirt appeal-ing. She's due to ring the doorbell at any moment (remember?), with any luck bearing gifts or at least her famous twelve-layer Jell-O salad. Hey, it's edible. Sort of.

Seventeen minutes have elapsed as you scuttle about the house, fling-ing baby stuff, newspapers, underwear, et al. into closets. You race to the nursery to check on the baby. Is he breathing? You place a hand on his chest and feel the blessed sensation of his tiny chest rising and falling.

Your precious wee one, all seven pounds and eleven ounces of him, is sleeping like a, well, like a baby, whatever that means. His arms are drawn close to his chest, and his knees are bent and curled up to his tummy. Your fingers itch to trace the outline of his tiny ear, and you want to plant a kiss on that darling nose. (All those relatives who swore Baby had Uncle Ivan's schnoz—well, they are out of their minds. Because Uncle Ivan clearly looks like Mr. Potato Head, and your son looks like…uh…unlike Mr. Potato Head.) Sigh. Isn't he the most spectacular sight you've ever laid eyes on? Daddy (as you've begun to call him) enters the room and puts his hand on your shoulder. Aunt Ethel fades to black.

Suddenly, the baby startles—or was that you?—and flings his arms upward with such a dramatic, almost violent motion you're sure he's going to start screaming. But no, he settles down within seconds, and you start breathing again. Daddy remarks that perhaps your son is Pentecostal, what with raising his hands so soon in life. You giggle. And then you start to tear up, for no other reason than that your milk came in the other day, and you feel a bit crazed.

Milk. How bizarre is it that all of a sudden, your body can produce a food item? It's like waking up one day and being able to get cheese out of your elbow or something. Come to think of it, cheese, being solid, would be a far sight easier to deal with than this milking business. Every two or three hours finds you plopped down somewhere with towels rolled under your arms, trying to cajole the little sucker to puh-lease latch on and partake so you don't have to call a hot line somewhere. Because, frankly, you don't have the energy to find that number for Lulu the Lactation Liaison.

Besides, you and your husband have become obsessed with poop. You're not out of the diapers-are-novelty-items phase yet, which means you actually don't mind changing them. The New Father, as he's referred to by neighbors and friends alike, was quite horrified by the meconium phase, that first week or two when Baby produced this black-green sticky substance so heinous it seemed to have come from the set of *Creature of the Deep* or some other horror flick. By now you're looking back almost fondly on the days of black and sticky, though, because now what you must contend with is yellow, squirty, and frequent (YSF). Or, if you're not breast-feeding, brown, squirty, and frequent (BSF).

 **Splish-Splash Sparingly**

Newborns shouldn't be bathed more than two or three times a week. They don't get dirty, and bathing them more often can dry out their skin.

Until the umbilical cord falls off (usually within two weeks), stick with sponge baths and don't get the stump wet. Use warm water (test it with your wrist), a soft washcloth, and just a little mild baby soap. Experts recommend using a "no tears" formula, since stinging eyes are no fun and such discomfort can pave the way for future bathtub battles.

Assemble everything you need before you begin. Then lay the baby on a safe surface and keep her covered with a towel except for the areas you're washing. For safety, have at least one of your hands on her body at all times. When you're done, cover her quickly, including her head, so she doesn't get cold.[2]

Is it safe to use wipes yet? Because they sure would be more convenient than those textured swaths of fabric soaked in warm, soapy water.
Aunt Ethel—oh dear! here in five minutes!—probably has an anecdote
about what kinds of swabbing materials (burlap sacks? old pillowcases?
straw?) were used in her day. Trust me; don't go there. And if your little
one is more than a week or two, I say ditch the hospital-issued do-it-
yourself-wipes-kit and indulge in a stack of prepackaged wipes. If your
baby's skin starts to get irritated, switch back. After all, you are performing
this little pants-changing ritual about seven to ten times a day, so the more
handy dandy the better.

## Your Kid Is a Big Crybaby

Face it. Baby Guido may very well be the offspring of wise guys, the long
awaited progeny of a long line of bodyguards, or the heir apparent to you
and your sumo-wrestler husband (you know, of the famous Italian Sumo
Wrestling Division), but he's still going to bawl his head off at the slightest
provocation. The average newborn cries two to three hours a day, peaking
at four to six weeks, then dropping off dramatically by the third month.

When he screams, you could take it to mean one of the following has
bent his itty-bitty psyche out of shape:

- The Munchies ("Feed me! Feed me!")
- The Messies ("I have just gone to the bathroom in my own
  pants, and to be candid, it doesn't feel so great.")
- The Gassies ("Yes, er, Mum, I seem to have a serious case
  of indigestion that needs your immediate attention.")
- The Suckies ("Here's how this works: I am full, true, but still
  rooting around looking for something to suck on. Please pop
  something in my mouth—a knuckle, a pacifier, my own clenched
  fist. This gives me a tremendous sense of well-being. Thank you.")

And of course, when all else fails, perhaps a tight burrito-style wrap will
calm the little *hijo* down. He misses the warmth, attachment, and security

of life in your womb, so do your utmost to recreate that close-knit atmosphere by wrapping him snugly.

You could also try some white noise. No, not the awful heavy metal band from the eighties, but a fan, a tape or CD of rain falling or waves, or a vacuum cleaner could work wonders, obliterating the excess stimuli that may have your little one tied up in knots. My friend Margaret said whenever her baby, Judah, got cranky, she just gave the living room a once-over. "As soon as that vacuum cleaner got turned on," she said, "there was silence."

## Rock-a-Bye Mommy

"Sleep when the baby sleeps" is as classic a piece of advice as you're apt to get, and it's a pretty good idea, too. There's only one problem: For a person who sleeps 80 percent of his day away, he seems to have little use for continuous slumber. Like the cat, which has been hiding behind the refrigerator since the baby's homecoming, short bursts of dozing are the order of the day, and night, for Baby. Junior is still only sleeping in two- to three-hour segments, maybe four or five if you're lucky, and six if you've won the Baby Lotto.

 **The Heart of Lullabies**

"The human heart beats sixty to eighty times a minute, at rest or during normal activity. Virtually all lullabies are composed within its rhythmic range, as if to replicate the experience of the womb."
—Rosanne Cash

So you look a bit like something out of *Creature of the Deep* yourself. Amy Einhorn, author of *The Fourth Trimester*, described her new mommy self: "I'm standing there having not showered, not been out of the house in a week, with bleeding, cracked nipples, and dark circles under my eyes that looked as if I'd swum the English Channel without remembering to take off my mascara."[3]

Your husband, naturally, looks fabulous, just a regular Mr. Haberdasher in his workday casual duds, without a trace of spit up (or worse). Having come off a week of paternity leave, he is now showering regularly, brushing, flossing, and enjoying a good six, seven hours of beautiful, luscious snoozing per night, while you haul your weary bones out of bed four times a night to dispense precious nutrients to his child. This is because you both agreed that you, being on maternity leave or possibly launching a new career as a stay-at-home mom, would get up with the baby at night, reasoning that he has to function at a rather sophisticated level in his position as a butcher, baker, candlestick maker, CPA, bus driver, welder, circus performer, or *whatever*.

This next part may alienate some of my male readers (whoever they might be), but it must be said: LET DADDY GET UP ON WEEKENDS WHILE YOU CATCH UP ON SLEEP. This will not only help him, as the child's other parent, bond with the baby, but also will aid you in avoiding: (a) a nervous breakdown, (b) falling asleep at the dinner table with your face planted directly in your mother-in-law's Tuna Temptation, or (c) typhoid.

My husband, Doyle, did this for me when both our babies were very young, and I'm convinced it went miles in preserving both my mental and physical health.

"Oh, but dear," I can hear your guy protesting now, "you're nursing. Like, exclusively! Am I right? So basically what I'm saying is, I'd love nothing more than to help ease your sleep deprivation, but I am simply forced to stay in bed because what can I do? As I said previously, you are nursing exclusively and, well, he'd be barking up the wrong tree with me, wouldn't he? Ba-ha-ha!"

Level him with your steeliest gaze and calmly suggest that, yes, you would still be feeding Baby, true, but that wouldn't necessarily exempt him from delivering Baby from the crib to your side. In this way you could just lie there while he does the fetching and probably the diaper duties afterwards.

If Junior is bottle-fed, you've got it made in the shade, as they say. TGIF just took on a whole new meaning!

But if today is only Tuesday and you're feeling it, that rather gaping hole in your life where REM was supposed to go, then do sleep when the baby sleeps. Even a couple of hours here and there throughout the day will mean the difference between sanity and psychosis. You'll probably be in a trance anyway, but there is a difference between the okay kind of trance, which is a bit woozy but still functional, and the bad kind of trance, which involves car accidents and other sleep-deprivation tragedies.

I was pretty much in the first kind of zombielike state after I had Ezra. In fact, on one occasion I had trouble remembering his exact name. My in-laws came over for a family Christmas get-together. (My C-section was five days before, and I couldn't quite muster the get-up-and-go to venture out of the house yet.) After a long but lovely evening, I bid everyone a good night. As I made my way up the stairs, my father-in-law, a good Grandpa but not great in the names department anyway, stumped me

 **Infant Jaundice**

Does your baby look a little yellow—not green—around the gills? She probably has infant jaundice, a condition affecting more than 50 percent of all normal, healthy babies in their first few days out of the womb. If she was born early, it may take a couple of months for her skin to be pretty in pink. What caused this yellow tinge? Baby's blood has too much bilirubin, a substance made during the breakdown of old red blood cells. Check with your doctor, who can determine whether your newborn needs treatment, such as phototherapy. Don't fret: Jaundice will pass quickly, and it usually does so without any special treatment.

when he said, in a spirit of warm, holiday cheer, "Good night, and thank you for Ira."

I paused, screwing up my forehead in an effort to truly think: *Did we name our baby Ira?* All I could conjure up was that guy from *Mad About You,* Paul Reiser's cousin. *Did we name our child after him? How strange.*

But then my mother-in-law elbowed her husband and hissed, "It's Ezra, not Ira," and I continued my painstaking journey up to bed, serene in the knowledge that, after all, we had not given our son a namesake from a sitcom now in syndication.

## Hold Me Gently, Rock Me Slowly

Babies love to be cuddled, and yours is no exception. One of the great pleasures of being a new parent is holding your little one close and just gazing. Gazing at his fluffy tuft of hair, receded not unlike Grandpa's to the back of his head. Gazing at his toes, just like Niblets of corn, only cuter. Gazing at his hands, like miniature starfish splayed on his chest.

We have a friend, Will, who upon congratulating us on the birth of our first baby, Jonah, urged us to grab on tight to every moment of our son's newness. "Soak in the preciousness of those newborn days," he wrote in the baby card. His own baby, Timothy, was already a big lug of six months old, and Will knew how fleeting the first moments are.

Newborns need warmth and cuddling. They crave those body noises and movements that became so cozy and companionable to him before he was born. So just sit there, anywhere, and absorb it all like a great big motionless 150-pound sponge (or whatever it is you happen to weigh, although I don't advise you to find that out just yet). Or, to flip metaphors for you, sop up the beauty and novelty and adoration as though you'll never experience this again—even if you likely will. Girlfriend, this is the gravy of life.

# On the Relationship Seat: Great-Aunt Ethel and Other Well-Meaning People in the Peanut Gallery

Here's how it went, your "conversation" with Great-aunt Ethel about the correct and proper methods to care for a baby:

Great-aunt E: "Isn't he just a little marvel? Why, I do believe he is the spitting image of your dear Uncle Ivan."

You: "Yes, um, well, thanks..." *I think.*

Aunt E: "What are you feeding him? I hope you haven't bought into this hippie notion of feeding him yourself, if you know what I mean."

You: "Myself? Well..."

Aunt E: "What I'm getting at, dear, is this newfangled claptrap about... Well, I think they are calling it 'nursing,' as if nursing had anything to do with it! Why, it's positively unsanitary! In my day, we boiled the dickens out of a bottle until it was absolutely hygienic—there's no way of boiling your feminine accouterments, now is there?"

---

 **Canapés and CPR**

If you didn't do this while you were pregnant, now's the time to sign up for infant CPR classes at local YMCAs, hospitals, community centers, or local American Red Cross chapters. Or you could get in on the new trend: "CPR Parties," where a certified instructor comes to your house and gives a five-hour class in both infant and child CPR. The American Red Cross asks for about three weeks' notice, and fees range from $25 to $45 per person. Nab a few newbie parent buddies and fix some snacks or have a potluck. Classes can be held with a minimum of six people and a max of twelve. For information, call your local American Red Cross or toll-free 1-800-667-2968.

You: "My feminine...huh?"

Aunt E: "And then we filled the bottle with canned milk and corn syrup, and by jingle! We knew precisely how much the wee darling was taking in. Please do close your mouth, dear! Why, you look as if you've seen a ghost! Anyway, none of this business of hoping the baby was getting enough! Why, these mothers today are starving their babies. It's a crying shame, that's what!"

You: "Oh."

Aunt E: "And another thing. In my day we were modest and decorous at all times. A lady wouldn't be caught dead flashing her assets in public, giving everyone a big show! I was telling Mildred at Bingo the other night—we don't play for money, dear, just points in the mail-order panty-hose club, so no need to look so shocked! Anyway, Mildred. I told her my niece was a sensible young woman and wouldn't be victim to some liberal gibberish. 'She's an old-fashioned girl, Millie,' I said. 'She'll feed my grand-nephew the way God intended—with a bottle—or my name isn't Ethel Maude Snodgrass!'"

So you thought you knew about the generation gap? When you became a mother, it probably widened considerably. There's only one Great-aunt Ethel, but millions of variations on the same basic model: people of a different era who did things differently. Between your mother-in-law's view that babies should sleep on their stomachs to avoid choking on spit up, and your retiree neighbor's insistence that you'll spoil that baby rotten if you pick her up every time she cries, you, like Lucy, have got a lot of splainin' to do. Tactful splainin', too, because the last thing you want to do is alienate those veteran mothers who—though they might cling to some outmoded ideas—are nevertheless your best source for mothering wisdom and practical tips.

Still, you and I, both being avid readers of baby magazines and books, know the truth about talcum powder (baby can ingest potentially harmful particles in her lungs), honey (can cause botulism), and the benefits of that bohemian breast-feeding business, but we don't have to get defensive about it. Yes, every comment and critique may make you feel as if you'd be better suited for work as a turnip farmer than somebody's mother, but who cares? Just blow it off. I know, that's easier said than done, but the truth is, you are his mother, not anyone else, and after even a few days spent caring for his every need, you know him better than anyone on the planet. Take any tips from well-meaning friends and relatives with a grain of salt, and remember who's ultimately responsible for Baby's well-being.

# The Top Ten Things Never to Say to a New Mom (and Oh-So-Tactful Comebacks)

### 1. "You're Not Breast-Feeding, Are You?"
Response: "Yup, I am. My pediatrician really encouraged me to try, and so far I think we're gonna make it."

### 2. "You're Not Bottle-Feeding, Are You?"
Response: "Uh-huh, I am, and it's been so wonderful for my husband to bond with the baby because he gets to share feedings."

### 3. "You Think You've Got It Rough. Well, Lemme Tell You About My First Month with Triplets!"
What you wanna say: "Did I ask you about your life with triplets? No. I didn't think so!" What you do say: "Wow. That must have been pretty wild. I have my hands full with one."

### 4. "Don't Eat That ——. It Will Get into Your Milk and Give the Baby Gas."
Response: "Really? Interesting. My lactation consultant said that every baby responds differently to various foods. If I notice any problems, I'll think about swearing off —— for a few days and see what happens."

### 5. "This Stuff (Sleepless Nights, Three-Hour Crying Jags, and So On) Is Nothing. Parenting Only Gets Harder from Here. Trust Me."

What you wanna say: "Stop speaking. Now. Or I shall be forced to yell in a primal fashion and then throttle you." What you do say: "Hmmm… That's what they say, don't they?"

### 6. "My Wife Came Home from the Hospital Wearing Her Old Jeans. Isn't She Something?"

What you wanna say: "I'm sorry. What did you say? The huge fat stores in my thighs are affecting my hearing." What you do say: "Yup, she's something all right."

### 7. "You're Not Scheduling Your Baby, Are You?"

Response: "Yes, I am. I did a lot of reading and asking around before the baby came and decided this was the best option for our family."

### 8. "You're Not Feeding on Demand, Are You?"

Response: Exactly the same as #7.

### 9. "You Look Tired."

What you wanna say: "Thank you. You look ugly. At least in a month or two I'll start looking like myself again." What you do say: "Ya think? Well, hopefully I'll start sleeping again real soon."

### 10. "When Are You Due?"

What you wanna say (and end up saying because all of your self-control has fled): "When are you due—for your lobotomy?"

My dear daughter Chloe Selah-Joy,

Can it really be that three months ago, even though you were in my tummy, I did not know you? Now it seems like you, at two months old, have always been here—you fit right into our routine. In the morning I wake up to your cry, and so I roll over and nurse you. Once your tummy is full, I prop you up on a pillow so I can look into your beautiful eyes, and then we talk. You grin and coo at me, and I smile and coo back at you. These times are one of the highlights of my day. You can't imagine the joy I feel when you smile at me with your eyes shining brightly. It makes all those nighttime feedings worth it.

I am so glad that you get all your nourishment from breast-feeding, and I love watching you when I'm preparing to nurse you. As I hold you on your side on my lap, you look anxiously from my face to my shirt yet wait patiently at first. Then you begin to pump your free leg and arm up and down. Finally it's latch-on time. Your brother and sisters are amazed at how you can latch on with your eyes closed. They ask, "How does she know where it is?" Then they get a little lesson on the powerful sense of smell that babies are born with. I love it when you reach out with your little hand and grab one of my fingers to hold while you nurse. That is so precious.

Just lately we've started to enjoy some playtime together in the afternoons. It is so fun to interact with you! I take your little hands in mine and do pat-a-cake with you. Oh, the look on your face—big grins, wide eyes, and head swaying even as you try to steady it in your excitement.

I am more and more convinced that while Daddy and I did not plan you, God did, and He knew what He was doing. He knows just what we need. I am so glad that God has graced our lives with you, a precious gift from Him. My prayer is that we will be able to train you in the Lord's ways, guiding you so as to help unwrap all the wonderful treasures He has stored up in you.

With much love always,

Mama

—Dawn Niewenhuise, mother of Reuben,
Naomi, Abigail, and Chloe

# The Blues, the Bellowing Baby, and Bums

*Milemarker!* This month all your TLC and sleep deprivation will be redeemed with that highlight of highlights: your baby's first real grin, a sight that will warm you head to toe. What a reward! You've been diapering, feeding, bathing, kissing, and cuddling without much response from your little human. But one day, between four and six or seven weeks, it happens: Your baby smiles, and you're sure she wasn't just tooting. Disarming, glorious, and wondrous, your baby's first authentic smile is as good as it gets.

## Blues Clues

In 1999, Marie Osmond gave birth to her seventh child, Matthew. Hit hard by postpartum depression, the smiling star's life as a wife, mom, and entertainer came to a grinding halt. As she describes in her book, *Marie Osmond: Behind the Smile,* some days she couldn't pull herself together, no matter what:

> I sit with my knees pulled up to my chest. I barely move. It's not
> that I want to be still. I am numb. I can tell I'm crying, but it's not
> like tears I've shed before. My eyes feel as if they have moved deep

into the back of my head. There is only hollow space in front of them. Dark, hollow space.... I can hear the breathing of my new-born son in his bassinet next to the bed. My ten-year-old daughter, Rachel, opens the bedroom door and, trying not to wake the baby, whispers, "Mom?" Not seeing me, she leaves. She doesn't even con-sider looking in the closet on the floor. Her mother would never be there.

She's right. The person sitting on the closet floor is nothing like her mother. I can't believe I'm here myself.[1]

While roughly 50 to 80 percent of new moms experience the "baby blues"—mood swings, irritability, and mild sadness—within the first ten days after childbirth, up to 20 percent develop postpartum depression (PPD), a major depressive illness that can occur at any time within a year of your baby's birth.

You may be at risk for PPD if you experience sensitivity to times of hormonal change, such as PMS or birth control pills, or if you have a per-sonal or family history of depression.

You may have PPD if the following is more than a fleeting thing and lasts more than two or three weeks:

- emotional instability, crying jags, anxiety, insecurity, feeling robotic and unreal, a feeling of shame and guilt over being a "bad mother"
- trouble concentrating, making decisions, sleeping, or eating
- sluggishness, fatigue, exhaustion
- memory loss
- overconcern for the baby
- irritability
- guilt, inadequacy, worthlessness
- lack of interest in the baby
- exaggerated highs and/or lows
- lack of interest in sex[2]

It's shocking, but those in the know estimate that up to 50 percent of all postpartum depression goes unrecognized—and thus undiagnosed—in doctor's offices.[3] That means that up to half of the new moms reading this book right now could have undiagnosed PPD!

And get a load of this canny observation: "There's a conspiracy of silence between ob-gyns and patients, a 'don't ask, don't tell' thing," says Dr. Diana Dell, M.D., an assistant professor of psychiatry and obstetrics-gynecology at Duke University Medical Center in Durham, North Carolina. "Women go to great lengths to cover up depression because there's a stigma associated with it. There's a lot of denial. People really want to see themselves as doing well."[4]

## On the Relationship Seat: The Ob-Gyn Worth Her Weight in Gold

At your six-week postpartum checkup, be open and honest about your emotional state. If you think you may have PPD, don't hesitate to discuss it with your doctor, who can and should help you.

 **Announcing: Zebulon Norman Snodgrass!**

Now that the blur of the first few weeks is clearing a bit, there's still time to send birth announcements. True, most people already know your baby was born, but birth announcements serve a more important function than sharing just the facts: They are fabulous keepsakes for years to come, especially if you invest some creativity in them. Not feeling particularly imaginative? Try www.amazingbaby announcements.com for easy solutions and cute ideas. The sweetest? Your baby's photo and stats printed on a Hershey's chocolate bar wrapper (also check www.hersheys.com for less expensive options).

After my first son was born, I definitely faked my well-being in front of my doctor, and I would have done so again after Ezra's birth, if not for two key reasons. First, my mom went through six years of severe and debilitating depression, so I knew a thing or two about the illness. Depression wasn't her fault, nor was it a sign of a weak spiritual walk. After watching her—an energetic cleaning maniac—become this silent person slouched in a chair, crying or staring through vacant eyes, I was convinced beyond a shadow of a doubt that her illness was just that, an illness. Watching my beloved mother walk this harrowing journey was for me a primer for accepting my own PPD.

Furthermore, as an adopted child, at first I thought my depression was not rooted in a genetic predisposition. But even after I discovered that the illness ran on both sides of my biological family, I was still shocked to realize I had it too, at least the postpartum version of it. But there it was, the feeling of being overwhelmed, out of it, snappish, and sad, so sad.

After three weeks, I went to see Dr. Gray for my "two week appointment." And this was my second key to facing my PPD: Dr. Gray looked me square in the eyeballs and said, "How are you doing emotionally?" I couldn't gloss over it, not with the pointed way she asked me.

"Well..." I hesitated for a couple of seconds and then spit it out. "I still feel kind of...sad."

Dr. Gray didn't mess around, and for that I will be eternally grateful. "We tell our patients that two weeks of baby blues is normal, but three weeks—it's PPD," she said. "Let's put you on a low dosage of Zoloft and see how that works."

Happily, I was among the 60 percent of PPDers who respond well to the first antidepressant they use. Zoloft worked with my brain chemistry—and that particular medication, along with Paxil, can be safely used during breast-feeding—and within three weeks or so I had more spring in my step.

For me, my mom's experience and my ob-gyn's mindful care were my saving graces.

Now, if you're worried about becoming dependent on an antidepressant, don't. Most PPDers only need to be on the medication for a few months to get them through the tunnel. You and your doctor can decide if and when you should drop the antidepressants.

If you feel as if your postpartum hormones have whacked you in the head, so to speak, please don't be shy about getting the help you need. You're not crazy, or anything close. Depression is a chemical loop-de-loop in your brain's neurotransmitters, not something you caused by not being good enough or stable enough or spiritual enough to withstand it.

As a new mom, you probably see your pediatrician more often than your ob-gyn. Many pediatricians are now being encouraged to watch for signs of PPD in their patients' mothers, so he or she may actually serve as quite an ally. Don't be afraid to mention your symptoms to your baby's doc or to any physician you see and feel comfy with. Even your friendly neighborhood podiatrist can probably give you a referral.

## Kick That Stigma in the Teeth!

Unfortunately, a bizarre stigma still attaches itself to depression, particularly in spiritual circles. My fair city boasts a church on just about every corner. It's a hamlet known for conservative values, a town proud of its stiff upper lip and hard-work ethic. This is a good thing, in many ways, but it can get kind of weird sometimes. For instance, according to Dr. Gray for one, many, many women who struggle with postpartum depression don't seek help. It's as if these new mommies are thinking, "I go to church every time the door opens, so what do I have to feel depressed about? I'll just pray more, and hopefully this thing will go away."

I won't lie to you. Some folks will think your canoe is a little tippy, that maybe you're not quite "up" to being a mother. That is *so* their problem! That a taint is *still* connected to all forms of mental illness, even pregnancy-induced bouts with PPD, strikes me as the goofiest thing in the world. But we can't control what other people think of us. All we can do is seek wisdom from our Father and do the best we can for our little families.

So here's my challenge to you: Be the most loving and caring new mom you can be by confronting your PPD head-on. Depression is bad for you, your marriage, and your baby. Take care of this thing, which is so, so treatable!

Would you accept medication and a doctor's care if you developed gestational diabetes? Well, duh! Take the bull by the horns here, girlfriend, and don't give a fig for what anyone thinks. You'll be your baby's hero—and mine.

In my effort to bolster the reputation and benefits of antidepressants, I don't want to neglect other helpful ways and means to treating depression. Exercise and diet have a huge influence on your body chemistry—thus your brain's chemicals too. I've heard that one good, vigorous thirty-minute workout can be the equivalent of an antidepressant in terms of raising your spirits. Consult a nutritionist about your diet if you need to, and stay away from the manic highs and crashing lows of megadoses of caffeine, sugar, and carbs. Talking to a therapist or a pastoral counselor who truly "gets" this stuff can also be wonderfully beneficial. Above all, reduce the obvious stress in your life if possible. Cut back on working long hours, resolve tangled and stressful relationships, and daily make it a practice to give up your burdens to the One who promises to carry them—your heavenly Father.

# Going Through the Big C (and I Don't Mean Chicago)

You're still kind of sore from your delivery and exhausted beyond belief. Still, all of this could be somewhat manageable, doable, were it not for your baby's screaming jags. Feel as though you're about to lose it? Colic will do that to you—make you feel as if you'd gladly give your left leg if only you could get your baby to stop yelling his head off for hours at a time. Jonah was a colicky baby, and I'll never forget the nights of rocking, burping, nursing, sticking a pacifier or my pinkie finger into his mouth—anything that might make a dent in the scream-a-thon. Sometimes I just couldn't take it anymore. I'd put my banshee baby in his swing, get in the shower, and cry my own eyes out, sure I was unfit for motherhood, loving my baby fiercely yet also resenting him. Doyle could handle the screaming a little better, but even his usually calm nerves were rattled.

Colic is hard on babies, but it's brutal on their parents. Listening to your baby cry for hours on end and trying to offer solace, often without any success, is downright burdensome, both physically and emotionally.

 ## The Soggy-Bottom Boys (and Girls)

You'll change about five thousand diapers over the next three years, around seven or eight per day now, and more like four to five when Baby turns one. Even if you try your utmost to keep your little one's buns dry and clean, he'll probably develop diaper rash at some point. I freaked out when Jonah all of a sudden had red splotches and swollen bumps all over his bottom. What was I doing wrong? Was I not changing him enough? I probably was doing everything right, in retrospect, but that first rash in particular can be unnerving for Mom and painful for Baby. The best advice I got on this topic was to coat the rash thoroughly with one layer of zinc oxide ointment, Bag Balm (yeah, it's for cows, but hey, Shania Twain uses it as wrinkle cream!), or petroleum jelly, topped off with a good dusting of powder. Powder's gotten a bad rap of late, but just make sure you use cornstarch rather than talc, and sprinkle it in your hand first before applying it so your baby doesn't breathe it in. This is one nasty mess, but the ultra-thick layer of goop provides a barrier between your baby's skin and wetness, and it truly works to heal the rash. Also, good old-fashioned air-drying after a warm soak can work wonders.

Typically, one in five babies will be afflicted with the Big C: Colic, a condition that generally starts when a baby is two to three weeks old and ends by age two or three months, when you're about ready for the men in white to take you to the rubber room. Experts say the worst of colic goes down when Baby's around five or six weeks of age.

Although no one's sure what causes colic, most in the know believe that colic is caused by sensory overload for a newborn. For some babies, the transition from the tranquil, dark womb world to the outside—lights, sounds, touch!—can be fraught with stress. In other words, the nervous system of colicky babies hasn't yet matured enough to filter all that's going on around them. With their still-weak shock absorbers, these little ones feel as if they're being shelled by stimuli and sensations, so by the end of the day (when most colic crying jags occur) they can't handle any more and need to let it all out.

If you're nursing, you may think Baby's colic is intensified when you chow down certain foods. Foods that turn Baby into Gassy Gus— allegedly—include coffee, cabbage, dairy products, and broccoli. But unless you're eating a whole head of broccoli and half a pot of Joe in one sitting, it's not too likely that your diet is the culprit. (And if you *are* eating a whole head of broccoli, that rubber room might be closer than we thought!)

Frankly, I don't buy the whole theory about foods getting in your breast milk and causing digestive commotion (see the chapter called "Feed Me First"). I know, I know: Cousin Cleo swore up one side and down the other that Baby Bruno simply could not tolerate her love for onions (actually, neither could anyone else), and when she gamely gave them up— *voila!*—Bruno was cured. Cured!

If it makes you feel better, by all means, keep a food diary. Note when your baby has his crying jags while keeping track of your diet, just to see if there's any kind of pattern. There's no proof that your eating habits can cause colic except in the most severe and rare cases. It's much more likely that the overstimulation theory is really true, which means that your baby needs you to dole out extra TLC, not to cut beloved broccoli from your diet.

Dr. Alan Greene, the go-to guy for colic, weighs in on some possible solutions:

> Some children are comforted by being held close in a dark room. Some like to be sung to. Some need to suck on something. Some are calmed by rocking. For many kids, car rides are settling. The motion moves the gas through and gently mesmerizes the child.

 ### Diaper Dollar Savers

- *Buy wholesale.* Warehouses like Sam's Club and Costco sell diapers by the case, slashing the prices you'll find at the grocery store.
- *Keep your eyes peeled for sales.* If you buy your diapers at the grocery store—and most people do—you can expect to be robbed blind by the end of your baby's diaper days. Your friendly neighborhood grocer is the most expensive place to buy diapers—except when they are on sale. Check those fliers. Occasionally, grocery stores will use diapers to entice you into the store, offering savings of 30 percent or more. (I just checked out the per-diaper price during a sale at Target: A ninety-six-count pack of diapers for $19.99 comes out to about $.20 per diaper! Stock up!)
- *Buy in bulk.* Skip those little packs of twenty diapers and look for 80- or 100-count packs to save 20 percent or more.
- *Click and save.* Web sites like www.diapers4less.com sell diapers at shockingly low prices. Sample price: $26.99 for a case of 204 newborn diapers. Even with shipping, that's a mere $0.17 per diaper.

Some children are intolerant to cow's milk–based formulas. Most of them will do well on soy, but about 20 percent of them are intolerant to soy as well. Nutramigen or one of the other hydrolysate formulas will often do the trick. Kids may not like them, but they are almost impossible to be intolerant to. Some parents do report relief from gas drops, especially if they are given at every feeding—not just four times a day.[5]

I wish I had figured out the gas drops thing before Jonah's colic. In Canada, we have a concoction of fennel seed oil called Gripe Water, which is supposed to calm a baby's turbulent tum tum. "They just have this big pepperminty belch, and they feel much better" was the assessment of one of my relatives. Certainly, there are gas drops stateside, too, though none with such a quaint name as Gripe Water!

## The Top Ten Parent-Tested Colic Busters

### 1. Wear Baby in a Baby Sling

This not only recreates the tightly wrapped coziness of the womb, but it also frees up your hands for dishes, thank-you notes, or Super Mario. If you don't have a sling, swaddle your baby snugly in a receiving blanket.

### 2. Play Peaceful CDs

Try playing CDs with soothing ocean sounds or soft music. Also, try one of those white-noise tapes of rainfall or restaurant din. (When it comes to getting Baby to sleep, white noise has its downside; more on that in Month Four. When it comes to colic, though, all bets are off. Do what works!)

The "Baby Go-to-Sleep Musical Therapy Series" is a collection of recordings set to the rhythm track of a human heartbeat, which can be heard as the baseline. "Alicia just *loved* these, both during her colicky phase and beyond," says Karen, whose daughter's colic lasted a solid three months. The first two products in the series contain classic nursery songs. The third is called "Jesus Loves Me Fast Asleep" and contains music tracks for Sunday-school classics such as "Into My Heart," "Jesus Loves Me," "Oh How I Love Jesus," "This Little Light of Mine," and so on. The cost is $12.95 each for cassettes, $24.95 each for CDs, plus $3.00 per order shipping and handling. To order by credit card or locate a store that sells the tapes, call toll-free 1-800-537-7748. Or mail check/money order to: Baby-Go-to-Sleep Center, P.O. Box 550, Colorado Springs, Colorado 80901.

### 3. Put Her in an Automatic Baby Swing or Take Her for a Car Ride

### 4. Take Baby Outside for a Walk

If the weather's not conducive to walking outside, try holding Baby firmly, standing on the floor, and bouncing gently from foot to foot. (Mini-trampolines work great too!)

 **The Dreaded Two-Month Vaccination**

I won't lie to you: Baby will hate the shots given to her at her two-month doctor's visit, but you'll hate them even more. One minute she's happy, cooing—life is good—and the next she looks at you in shock and outrage: "Mommy, how could you let them do this to me?" You'll feel terrible, of course, but try to focus on the wonderful benefits of vaccines and how they will protect your baby from horrible illnesses. In a few minutes, the storm of screams will have passed—and Baby will feel much better too! For the two-month round of shots, expect a dosage of DtaP (diphtheria, tetanus, and pertussis), Hib (haemophilus influenza, type B), PCV (pneumococcal vaccine), and probably a second dose of the hepatitis B vaccine.

## 5. Place Your Baby in a Baby Seat on Top of the Clothes Dryer

Keep your hands on the baby seat to prevent it from vibrating off the edge of the dryer. The combined motion and white noise may soothe her.

## 6. Employ the Vacuum Cleaner or Run Water in the Bathtub

Jonah occasionally calmed down when I laid him on the fluffy bath mat near the tub while the water ran. These moments were sheer bliss.

## 7. Set Your Baby in Front of an Aquarium

The bubbling sound from the aerator and the movement of the bubbles are calming.

## 8. Hang Tight

Experts urge parents to stick with a method for five minutes for best results. Don't give up on one method too quickly. If after five minutes the baby is still crying, don't get discouraged—just move on to the next strategy.

## 9. Take Mini-Vacations

For your sanity, make sure you take mini-vacations from coping with Baby's colic. Trade off with your husband so you can take a walk or a hot shower. Accepting the offer of a grandparent, friend, or relative to come over and hold your child for a few hours doesn't mean you can't hack it as a mom. Well, maybe you can't hack the ceaseless, nerve-frying crying, but who can? Arranging for a backup plan makes you a resourceful and realistic parent, and both you and Baby will benefit.

My cousin's second child was a screamer, and she occasionally deposited her shrill offspring at her mom's for a few hours of peace. If you think the grandparents or your sister-in-law can cope with a couple of hours of ear-piercing bedlam, ask for their help. After all, second to you and the new pa, they adore Baby, even when she's bellowing blue murder. You'll find that you can handle Baby's colic better if you're not a woman on the edge, and some peaceful pockets of time will help you go the distance with this season of colic.

## 10. Above All, Pray

Unload your frayed, shell-shocked self to your Father in heaven. "Cast all your anxiety on him because he cares for you" (1 Peter 5:7). Ask Him for patience, calm, and the ability to help you endure. Ask Him for a measure of His unconditional love to surround you and your baby. Thank Him again for the gift of your precious little one and for the constancy of His patience and love for you.

Remember, this too shall pass. It really, truly will. I promise. Before you know it, your baby's colic will end, perhaps just as abruptly as it started. And when it does, you'll fall in love with your now-smiling, cooing bundle (scream—who me?) all over again.

Good Morning, Sunshine,

You, Josephine, just celebrated your three-month birthday, and each new day with you is a celebration. I love you more than I can express with words, hugs, kisses, or physical care. And I feel as if you have always been here. I can't imagine a day without you. One year ago the Lord began to knit your little body and personality inside of me. Even back then, He had a plan for you. I can't wait to see what it is!

Every morning, you call out to me with your funny sounds. (I'm not quite sure if you realize you are making them yet. When you "speak," you appear a bit surprised at your "words.") I then open your door and call back to you. We chat a bit before I come in, and then the sun rises in our house. Your smile, my sweet girl, melts my heart every time you flash it.

I can already see many qualities in you that you have inherited from either Daddy or me. You already love books, and you love to talk (a trait from me). Sometimes I think that you know much more than we think you do when you stare intently at the hinges rather than the toy bar on your baby swing. Maybe one day you'll be a scientist like your daddy.

Your giggle, Josephine, is priceless. I find myself spending hours in attempts to pry it out of you. Never has there been such a blissful sound. I know it will only continue to grow more endearing.

You are loved by so many people, little one. You are a gift from the Lord to your extended family. When your Papa [grandfather] passed away two months before your birth, the Lord intended that you would help to fill the cavernous hole left by his departure. You have Papa's delightful, loving, spirited character, and I pray that you will have his integrity and love and devotion to his Lord. He was a great man, and you will hear about him all of your days. Even though he is gone to be with the Lord, you will learn volumes from him.

I love you, my darling, my daughter, my delight. I always will.

Love,

Your Mommy

—Mary Jo Haab, mother of Josephine

# The Trance, a Moon Dance, and Pediatric Assurance

*Milemarker!* Incredible stuff: Your baby's brain—and yours—has this gadget called the parietal lobe, which manages hand-eye coordination and allows us to recognize objects and people. That piece of gray matter is developing like crazy right now. On a parallel track, his temporal lobe, another chunk of the brain, is quickening his hearing, language, and olfactory senses. Working together, these smart lobes are your baby's touchstone for hearing your voice, knowing it's you, and responding more interactively. This is the beginning of a beautiful relationship!

## The 24/7 Stupor Thing

I am a world-class sleeper and I am not ashamed. Shuteye, for me, is one of the best gifts in life, an opportunity to rest my weary bones, snuggle in soft bedclothes (isn't that a great old-fashioned term, bedclothes?), and basically retreat to a quiet, peaceful world.

For me, the gold standard of slumber is sleeping in, as in waking naturally, no alarm blaring in my ear, leisurely regaining consciousness at my own pace. Motherhood, therefore, was a bit of a shock to my system.

To my horror, not only did I forgo, maybe forever, the luxury of sleeping in, but I also was called upon to rouse myself out of my bed—during the night!—to tend to the needs of a squalling infant. It was a blow, to be sure.

Right about now you're probably craving sleep like a trying-to-quit smoker longing for nicotine, thirsting for rapid-eye-movement sleep like a dehydrated runner hankers for a bottle of Dasani. You've heard of walking pneumonia? Serious lack of sleep, such as that experienced by new moms and dads, is a walking coma.

Writer Nell Bernstein had double the sleep deprivation when she started parenthood with twins. She remembers well the 24/7 stupor thing:

"The list of things no one tells you before you become a mother is fairly exhaustive—in part because nature arranges for us to forget the hardest parts so we'll remain open to the prospect of doing it all again; in part because experienced mothers knew if we told the whole, unadulterated truth, it might well mean the end of the species. But for me, no part of new motherhood was as shocking, as overwhelming, as the cumulative impact of sleep loss.... The lowest point came when I nearly stepped in front of a bus because I was so disoriented."[1]

## It's a Marvelous Night for a Moon Dance

Your friends, family, and coworkers—those sans babies themselves—may find it difficult to understand why a newborn who sleeps sixteen to twenty hours a day would be so subversive to your sleeping life. But we grownups need unbroken, sustained sleep. Even if you're monumentally fortunate enough to snag eight hours, if they're disconnected frequently enough by Mr. Spasmodic Sleep, then they don't count as premium rest. That would make them...low-quality rest. See how that works? And that's not a good thing.

Where things really go haywire is when sleep loss goes on and on, for weeks and months. Unlike an episode of insomnia, chronic REM deprivation can wreak havoc on you until you're no longer sure your body and soul are headed in the same direction.

You may not step in front of a bus, like Bernstein, but experts say habitual loss of quality sleep can play around with your memory (gee, where *did* those keys get to?), make a normally decisive person wishy-washy, and take the wind out of your creative sails.

If you're seriously doze-deprived as I was, one of the most distressing by-products is lack of what the experts call "emotional regulation." It's harder to keep it together, and it shows. The downward spiral continues when you add precarious hormones to the equation. Put a nonsleeping, estrogen-whacked new mom in the ring with Mike Tyson, and I would have to pick the new mom. Things could get a little loopy in your marriage, too. If you wonder why all of a sudden you're this screechy, blubbering mess, here's one clue: YOU NEED MORE SLEEP.

If you've just plunged into motherhood for the first time, chances are you are hardest hit by sleep forfeiture. Overwhelmed by the colossal needs of your new baby and being somewhat of a greenhorn at this motherhood business, you may truly be at a loss as to how to manage your infant's sleep needs and your own.

My number one piece of advice to you is this: Consider your own sleep needs as seriously as you consider your baby's. Life will become much, much more manageable that way, I promise. In addition to baseline functioning, with more siesta time you'll remember your best friend's phone number, be able to tell her, "No, I cannot host a Tupperware party for you," and maybe even rearrange the living room in an attractive fashion.

## The Top Ten Ways to Sleep Like a Baby (Without Waking Up Crying Every Two Hours)

Here are a few more ideas to get you the snooze you can use:

### 1. Share Night Duty

If you're breast-feeding exclusively, you and your guy can still share night duty when you pump. Yeah, Daddio may have to be up and at 'em early for work, but as my friend Lisa points out, Mom's doing valuable work too. More and more new parents are opting for the split shift, keeping in mind that the baby is both of their offspring, so they should be sharing the sleep loss too. Work out a plan where you hit the sack at about 9:30, and your mate gives Baby a bottle of formula or expressed breast milk the first time he wakes up. Then you're on the "second shift" covering the rest of the night. That way you both get a five- or six-hour unit of high caliber sleep, plus a few shreds of dozing through the night. Your guy might complain about being bleary-eyed for the staff meeting or whatever. At this point it may be prudent to tell him the "New Mom Almost Gets Squashed by Bus" story.

## 2. Get Away—at Least a Few Feet

Close yourself off from the world: Sleep in the guest room—or put Dad on the sofa.

## 3. Let a "Night Nurse" Help Out

This may seem a little extreme, but you might want to take people up on their offers to help by suggesting that they volunteer as night nurses. This plan will work better with, say, your college-aged sister or your retired parents than a pal with six munchkins of her own to get bleary-eyed over.

## 4. Get Yourself a "Nap Nanny"

I *so* wish I had tried this: Employ a "nap nanny"—a friend, relative, or neighbor who has a clue about babies—and then hit the sheets *hard* for two or three or four hours. (Baby will be fine!)

## 5. Leave the Early Morning Feedings to a Family Member

Let your parents or your in-laws do the early morning feeding so you can sleep in a little.

## 6. Leave the Building

A more extreme measure, yes, but your sanity is probably worth it. Go to a hotel and sleep for ten solid hours. Leave Junior in the capable hands of his doting dad or, if you and Hubby want to take your sleep-in vacation as a pair, with Grandma and Grandpa.

## 7. Turn Off the Monitor

There's no way you can get any decent rest when you can hear Baby every time she grunts, twitches, snores, or moves her arm. You need sleep! Baby needs you to sleep! Bury the monitor in the backyard if you have to, but don't leave that thing on—whatever you do! Don't worry, you'll hear the little tyke when he really wakes up. (If you can't bear to be incommunicado with Baby, don't blame me when your own personal "bus" hits.)

## 8. Schedule Exercise

Get moving during the day, so that your bod is good and tired when your little one sleeps. More on that in Month Seven.

 **You Wouldn't Drive Drunk, So Don't Drive Drowsy**

Researchers in Australia and New Zealand report that sleep deprivation can have some of the same hazardous effects as being drunk.

"Getting less than six hours a night can affect coordination, reaction time and judgment," they said, posing "a very serious risk."

Drivers are especially vulnerable, the researchers warned. They found that people who drive after being awake for 17 to 19 hours performed worse than those with a blood alcohol level of .05 percent did.[2]

## 9. Let Baby Sleep Close By

When Baby is really little, like bassinet size, have her sleep at arm's reach. True, I just badgered you to turn the monitor off, but maybe a white noise machine or fan could blot out her "nothing serious" noises. This way you don't even have to get out of bed. You can just roll over and gather your hungry bundle to your bosom—you're both good to go. She's eating and you're dozing. Everyone wins. I did this with Ezra, and I highly recommend this.

Bottle feeders, you could try one of those nifty new thingamabobs that keeps a bottle cool then, with a flick of a switch, warms it up perfectly for feeding. Or how about keeping a sterilized bottle on your nightstand, with dry formula inside, and a bottle of purified water. Then you just have to pour the water in the bottle, shake, and again, it's all good.

The point is, obviously, staying in your dark, warm bed and not waking up so fully that it becomes challenging to fall back to sleep. Some people vow that keeping a baby in one's bedroom is bad because then, the logic goes, you'll never get Baby to sleep in his own room. Well, I disagree. My babies both spent the first few months in bassinets and made a smooth transition to their own cribs. (More on getting Baby to sleep in Month Four.)

## 10. Give Up the Stimulants

If you haven't already, give up the caffeine and avoid as much sugar as you can during this season. Both caffeine and sugar are stimulants that can interrupt your sleep cycles as often as a baby's cry. Eat a meal high in protein before dozing for sweet, sweet ZZZs.

# On the Relationship Seat:
# Fido and Felix

When Doyle and I were yet on the cusp of parenthood, we were the owners of one pet, a four-year-old Siamese cat named Pierre. Having raised

## Pediatric Reassurance

Dr. Akourkour Addy, my sons' very own pediatrician, is perhaps the best baby doctor on planet earth. (Okay, so I exaggerate, but she truly is marvelous. Here's hoping that you have or can find a physician as reassuring, wise, and nurturing as ours is. See "Finding a PHAT Pediatrician" on page 60.) Born and raised in Ghana, Dr. Addy also brings the valuable—and not often heard—perspective of African culture and traditions to raising and caring for a new baby. Here's what she had to say:

*Q: Your "specialty" is brand-new moms. Why do you think bringing home a newborn is so daunting, even for new parents who have achieved great success in the workplace?*
A: It's very scary. This baby is a real live person, and you're responsible for it. Whether you're in the medical profession or not, you see that this baby is a person whose needs have to be met by you, and you want to do as good a job as you can. It can be intimidating.

*Q: What's the difference between first-time and second-time moms?*
A: I always say that the first baby is for worrying about; the second baby is for enjoying. Second-time moms come in very relaxed, telling me how easy their baby is and how much fun they are having. First-time moms are typically very anxious. They call me saying, "My baby isn't sleeping enough" or "My baby is sleeping too much," even if their babies are very much within the normal range of development. But there's no way around it. You have a big learning curve with the first baby. In developing countries, there is a much stronger support system for new parents. You are surrounded by relatives who can help you, and most likely you will have experience around little babies—your nieces and nephews and cousins. In the United States, many times the grandparents are far away, and moms don't get the support and reassurance they need, so they call me.

*(continued on next page)*

*Q: I've read that there is a new emphasis on "family pediatrics." That is, pediatricians are encouraged to be alert for things like postpartum depression in the mother, which can affect the entire family.*

A: Yes. I always ask the mom, "How are you doing?" [Our appointments are] not just about the baby. I say, "Do you have enough support?" Sometimes these questions help the mom open up, and sometimes they are very emotional and I can tell they probably have PPD. I always tell them, "You didn't do anything wrong. You didn't get depressed because you weren't strong enough or because there was sin in your life." A lot of moms feel ashamed. They think they are not supposed to whine about themselves. Maybe their church teaches that any mental illness is a sin. But this is biological, a result of hormone imbalance, and it's very treatable. By not getting help, moms are doing their babies a disservice. If a mom is not functioning well, the home is in chaos, and the whole family suffers. Some moms don't want to tell me because they think they will have to stop breast-feeding, but there are quite a few medications that are compatible with nursing—totally safe.

*Q: I've heard you say, jokingly, that if one of your kids married someone who didn't believe in vaccines, you would kidnap your grandchildren and have them immunized. Why do you feel so strongly?*

A: I do feel strongly about vaccines. There is so much information out there today, especially on the Internet, which isn't quite accurate. People believe what they read, and they think there is a link between, say, autism and vaccines. I believe it's very unlikely that there is such a link, though we don't yet know what does cause autism. But having your children immunized is a big part of caring for their well-being.

*Q: How do you reassure new parents?*

A: I say, "Don't panic over little things." They want to do a good job, and if they are trying their best, it's going to be okay. I always address what they can expect in terms of their baby's development between appointments. "Next month he will start to roll over, or sit up, or pull to a stand." That way they can watch for these things. I encourage moms and dads to call me between appointments with questions. It is a long process to raise a baby until he is eighteen, but I always point to the Bible: "Train a child in the way he should go, and when he is old he will not turn from it."

Le Chat since kittenhood—when we adopted him out of a shotgun shack and a certain life of bourgeois, which we remind him of when he gets too uppity—we were attached to him, despite his flaws. (Okay, okay, so I was the only one remotely attached to Pierre. At times I was the only thing standing between life and death for that cat.)

I was raised with a Siamese cat—Toby—so I was familiar with the smug stares, the "I'm the king of the castle" karma, and the "Oh puh-lease" response to any kind of attempt at affection. The Siamese arrogance struck me as humorous; at least they had a personality, which seemed to be somewhat lacking in many cats of my acquaintance. So I thought I

 ### Finding a PHAT (Pretty Hip and Terrific) Pediatrician

One of the most vital relationships you have as a new mom is with your pediatrician (or family doctor). You need to find someone who will answer your questions—and there will be many of those over the first year—and give you satisfactory answers. It's nice to have a doc with a warm and fuzzy bedside manner, but it's not necessary. What is imperative is that you hitch your baby's health wagon to a trustworthy, competent, and reassuring physician. Here are a few thoughts to keep in mind when choosing your baby's doc.

- Obviously: Does your insurance carrier cover this doc's office?
- Most doctors have only about ten to fifteen minutes to spare for an interview. Don't bend the poor guy's ear so long he'll have to charge for the privilege.
- Find out who covers for her when she's not available. A group practice is great because you know someone will be on-call to answer your middle-of-the-night concerns, even if your doctor's sunbathing in Baja.

knew what I was getting into with Pierre. I was wrong. This cat is the crankiest feline ever to pad around planet earth. And that description comes from someone who is kind of fond of him. Pierre has bitten the children of dinner guests, left tooth marks on my ankles so many times they are now permanent, and once sent the mailman to a med center to be treated for scratches. But other than that he's really very cuddly.

All that to say, when we contemplated bringing our already much-loved baby home, we wondered how our feisty feline would respond. Would the blue-eyed menace become a green-eyed monster? We were quite worried. Basically, we made the decision to "deal with" Pierre if he ever acted aggressively towards Jonah. We weren't concerned, though, that

- Ask about evening and weekend hours and about how to reach him or one of his partners in an emergency.
- Find out where your doctor stands on the Big Choices, such as bottle-feeding, breast-feeding, sleep training, antibiotics, and vaccines. If you significantly disagree with your doctor on one or more of her views, you may want to avoid friction now and find a more compatible medic.
- When you visited the pediatrician's office, did you wait a long time? Was the place clean and orderly? Did the waiting room and examination rooms offer toys and books to keep Junior busy while you waited? Was the nurse you dealt with more of a Florence Nightingale or a Nurse Ratchett?
- The single most valuable piece of advice I can give you on finding a doctor is to do so through a pal's referral. If your girlfriend passionately endorses her baby's doctor—as mine did and I do now—chances are excellent that you will find a welcoming and compatible medical home for you and your little family too.

our cat would cause our baby to suffocate by lying on top of him. That seemed altogether unlikely behavior from Pierre, who only purred when he was really in the mood to purr, and only then when rubbing his face on Doyle's beard. (You see, Pierre thinks Doyle is his mother, I'm convinced. Doyle will roll his eyes when he reads this.) He is not an animal given to untoward displays of affection.

Surprisingly, and much to my relief, Pierre ignored Jonah for the first few months of his life, occasionally stooping to a quick whiff of baby skin before sitting four feet away, observing the newest Craker through slanted eyes. When Jonah started to crawl at six months, he sped after Pierre every chance he got, absolutely delighted with the family pet, such as he was. To Pierre's credit, he stayed out of Jonah's way, not showing any interest in being clutched by chubby little fists.

I've heard of family cats that allow their household babies to man-handle and maul them without twitching a whisker. Or other cats that simply take to living nocturnal lives, emerging from a safe, baby-free spot when the last munchkin has been tucked in for the night.

When Jonah could actually catch Pierre, which wasn't easy, things became a little more dangerous. Soon, though, our busy boy learned to exercise caution with the cat. A couple of swipes from Pierre gave Jonah an invaluable lesson in approaching all animals with care.

Hopefully, your kitty is a little more gentle than ours. Actually, I've never heard of a cat so ornery as Pierre, so it's pretty safe to assume your cat's going to be okay with the baby.

Dogs are a different story. We got ours about four months before Ezra was born, and I'm still adjusting, nineteen months later. Dinah is a chubby two-year-old basset hound who came to our house vis-à-vis Blanche and Roy, this pregnant couple we met in the baby name section of Borders. I have to be honest and say this pooch gets on my last nerve. Not only does she shed massive amounts of dog hair everywhere, but her ability to bark her head off at the slightest provocation and run out the door down the street, mindless of my yelling her name, has caused no small amount of annoyance on my part.

Doyle adores Dinah. He talks baby talk to her the minute he walks in the door after work. It's enough to make you sick, that's what. But her one saving grace, in my mind, is that she is good with the kids. Well, she did knock poor Ez over a few times when she was on one of her "I'm so agitated by that squirrel on the deck that I am going to run from one end of the room to the other as fast as I can" rampages. But on balance, she's gentle and easygoing, even when a particular tot is poking her in the eye or sitting on her belly or stepping on her ears.

 **Photo Firsts!**

Here are some fun "firsts" for you to capture on film—and on your calendar. Whether or not you scrapbook, you won't want to forget these unmissable moments!

- trip to the park
- visit to Grandma's
- first solid food (Try to snap the pic during that window of opportunity when Baby isn't flinging his pureed squash at you!)
- tooth
- favorite toy
- baby-sitter
- fancy-schmancy event, like Easter or Baby's baptism or dedication
- time spent with a pal and her new baby (Sure, all the two of them do is loll around and drool on each other. But you and your best friend, the other baby's mother, can tell Gus and Max will be inseparable from this moment on!)

Dogs, though, are supposed to be more jealous of babies than cats are. My theory is that cats are just too stuck up; it doesn't even occur to them to be jealous. Irritated, yes. Envious, no.)

## Prepare, Quadrupeds, to Be Usurped

"The family pet," says writer Trisha Thompson, "is a territorial creature, and he'd prefer to maintain his status as your one and only 'child' and retain all the affection that Alpha Mommy and Daddy have to give."[3]

Pet preferences being what they are, our furry friends are going to have to deal with reality. Here are some tips to help them cope:

### Clothing for Sniffing

Experts say that you should bring an item of Baby's clothing home for Fido to sniff before you bring the actual baby. The dog or cat should be able to immediately discern that the baby is a member of their "tribe" or "pack," which means they will most likely show Junior the same affection—or disdain—that they show you and your husband.

### Babies for Sniffing

With careful supervision and parental approval, have your dog or cat sniff one or more babies in the weeks leading up to your delivery. Ideally, have your pet as accustomed as possible to babies before you bring yours home.

### New Doggie Digs

If the pet is likely to get ejected out of the family bed to make room for Baby, break him in gently by introducing cozy, new doggy digs before Baby takes his spot.

### Pet Screens

If your cat is very affectionate, it might be a good idea to buy one of those pet screens that attach to Baby's crib so there's no chance of the cat smothering Baby in her sleep. You never know how your cat will react to Baby, so for the first few weeks and months, make sure he's banned from Baby's sleeping quarters, just in case.

## Lots of TLC

Make sure your fleabag and fluffball know that they still hold a special place in your heart. Give them lots of TLC when Baby's napping or when someone else is holding her. They'll soon get the picture that, true, life as they knew it will never be the same, but this new biped (future biped) ain't half bad. Hey, in a few months, the pets will love chasing airborne chunks of food being flung off the highchair, and they'll wonder why on earth you two didn't get one of these mini-owners sooner.

## A Note About Allergies

Of course, you'll have no idea if your baby is going to be allergic to your pets before you have her. Keep her room well ventilated and ban the pets as much as you can. If Baby shows signs of allergies—red, itchy, watery eyes, a rattle in her chest, frequent ear infections—get with your pediatrician and try to hammer out the cause of the symptoms: colds or allergies? Be prepared to part with your pooch or kitty, if—in extreme cases—Baby's misery is due to pet dander.

My Sweet Lou,

I loved you from the moment I saw you, and each day I can feel my love grow bigger and bigger. Here you are, already four months old, but we are still just beginning to get to know each other. Each morning I wonder, "What new things will my Little Lou learn today?"

You are such a content baby, sitting in your little chair or lying under your toy arches. Lately when you are on my lap and I pull you up to sitting or standing, you just break out in your little laugh. It is so cute, my heart just melts. You are starting to talk to me, too. We have long conversations together. You open your mouth in a cute little O and let your tongue move in waves as you make all sorts of sounds—long ones, short ones, high ones, squeaky ones. And then you laugh and reward me for acting so goofy! I hope you think I'm half this funny when you are a teenager.

We did not find out if you were a boy or girl at the mid-pregnancy ultra-sound, so it was a big surprise when I delivered you. When I first saw that you were a boy, I felt the strong sense that God gave you to Daddy and me because He knows how desperately this world needs men of integrity and strong moral character. I believe that you will grow up to be this kind of man. I pray for the strength and wisdom to raise you so that you will be equipped to fulfill God's call on your life. It's an overwhelming thing to tell a four-month-old, but we'll take it one day at a time, I promise!

You are such a honey! Your cheeks are getting chubbier by the day, and I can't help but kiss them over and over. Luckily, you don't seem to mind very much. I know that you will soon squirm out of my lap and try to get away, so I am savoring these moments with you, these quiet moments when you nuzzle your soft head by my chin and let me hold you still and close.

I love you very much, Louis,

Mommy

—Suzanna Breems, mother of Henry and Louis

# Sleeping, Scheduling, and a Swell Connection with the Doc

*Milemarker!* Prepare to be amazed: Just when you thought your little guy couldn't get any more remarkable, he flipped from his front to his back! You thought you saw that one coming, what with the minipushup thing (where he hoisted his head and shoulders, using his muscular little arms for support), but your baby's first real roll was a WOW moment for the whole family. Most munchkins flip from front to back first, but the other way is cool, too. (Note: Don't fret if Baby isn't rolling yet. Some babies never really roll over. They skip that breakthrough and move right on to sitting, lunging, and crawling.)

## Good-night, Baby!

Paul Reiser's book *Babyhood* has definitely provided loads of yuks around here as we delve into his hilarious take on the state of new parenthood. One of my favorite stories in his book is his "lust for sleep" bit. Of being an exhausted new dad, Reiser wrote, "I didn't realize how extensive the change was till I found myself one day staring at a lingerie ad with a beautiful, seductive young woman sprawled...across a satin-sheeted bed, and all I could think was, 'Man, that bed looks comfortable.'"[1]

Can you relate? It doesn't take long at all for new parents to develop a carnal, wanton need for slumber. Sometimes our babies cooperate, sometimes they don't.

By now you have probably chosen a "type" of sleep training for your baby: the "schedule-your-baby" philosophy, the "feed and sleep on demand" approach, or something in between. My friend Meredith is a scheduler all the way, and we'll hear from her momentarily. Patti, on the other hand, has taken a different path: "I *never* fed my babies on a schedule. I don't eat on a schedule when I'm hungry, so why would I force my infant child to do something I wouldn't do myself? I do not think that an infant needs to be on a schedule. I think most mothers do that for their own convenience, not for the health of the child."

Whew! Them's fightin' words! Patti's strong opinion does illustrate the fact that few people are neutral on this topic, present company (meaning me) excluded. With Jonah, I was so shell-shocked by new motherhood that I was clueless about the different sleeping (and feeding) ideas out there. I just fed him when he seemed hungry, tucked him in for a nap or a sleep when he seemed drowsy, and hoped for the best. When my first-born fell into sleeping through the night—meaning eight hours or more—at about eight weeks of age, I secretly thought his early snoozing was a sign of his giftedness—and mine. Then I had Ez, who slept through the night at, oh, about nine or ten months.

But whether you buy into scheduling or choose—intentionally or not—a more laissez-faire approach, those in the know insist that there are methods to this madness, ways for the walking dead among us to get the little live wires to lapse into la-la land for longer stretches of time. At six to eight weeks, say the experts, babies commence sleeping in predictable four- to six-hour blocks of time at night. According to your pediatrician, the technical definition of "sleeping through the night" may mean snoozing from about midnight to 6 A.M. I know I'm not a doctor, or even a dental hygienist for that matter, but puh-lease! Six hours is "the night"? I wanna know who died and made these people in charge of what constitutes a full night of sleep! The whole thing sounds fishy to me, and I refuse to buy into it! If they added even an hour or two to those measly six, I would be happier about the whole thing.

That off my chest, here are some reality-tested tips for getting Junior to hit the sheets regularly and for more than a couple of hours at a stretch—maybe even eight hours straight.

## No Dozing

By four to six weeks, try not to let Baby doze off completely while you're rocking or feeding her. Otherwise, she won't ever fall asleep unless you're rocking or feeding her, and that's not good. No one wants to become a giant human pacifier. "But oh no, no, no," you may complain. "Rocking my baby at night is just too sweet and wonderful to give up, even for decent shuteye." So true. The trick isn't to drop the cozy rock-a-bye-baby times; instead, just try tucking her in her crib while she's drowsy but still awake. That way she won't become dependent on you for falling asleep. Once your baby has the hang of drifting off on her own, you can wake her for a feeding right before you're ready to hit the sack yourself. She'll most likely linger later in the morning and won't wake you for a snack just as you're nodding off.

## Moving Baby Out

When he's posed for his first studio portrait, it's time to move him out the door. Don't worry. He's just down the hall. At three months or so, you should brace yourself for letting Baby sleep in his own bed, as opposed to the bassinet by your bed or beside you. After that, experts say, it's much harder to make the move since he'll be in the habit of having you nearby. I know this won't be easy. I believe I cried the first night there was a gaping space beside my bed where that ruffled bassinet used to be. I missed my baby! But if you don't plan on the cosleeping life, it's time for The Switch. You could always pull a Linus (remember him, that adorable, blankie-toting boy in the Peanuts cartoons?) to help make the transition from cosleeping to independent snoozing a little easier.

Trade an article of clothing so he seems closer to you and you seem closer to him. After all, they say even newborns are soothed by their mother's scent. Pick a lightweight piece of clothing like a T-shirt—nothing too cushy or bulky—and place it in the crib with your little one. He may just be comforted by the thought that he's sleeping near you, even if you are really in your own bed. You, meanwhile, can cuddle up with a pair of Baby's pj's or a romper. If your husband makes fun of you, tell him to go sleep on the couch.

### Consistent Ritual

"Consistent bedtime rituals signal it's time to go to sleep," says Jodi Mindell, author of *Getting Your Baby to Sleep*. She advises sleep-happy parents to keep their routines brief, no more than thirty minutes, so it's clear bedtime is coming. You might want to feed your baby, change her, then read her a story, and rock or massage her.[2] I hung a musical toy off Ezra's crib as soon as he was sleeping regularly in his crib, and I played it at bedtime. The lullaby, "Go to Sleep My Dear Baby," seemed to trigger the whole idea of slumber in my baby's brain.

My friend Margaret has found great success with the sleep-rituals concept: "Zion and Judah were miracle babies when it came to the whole internal clock thing. I would like to take all the credit, but with them sleeping eight to ten hours a night at seven weeks, it is nothing short of a miracle," she says. "The one point I will add to my scoreboard is that I was a pretty consistent mom when it came to certain routines. Their crib was the only place I would purposefully put them down when it came to naps and bedtime. They sort of got the picture that their cribs equaled sleep. Now I wasn't insane, mind you. I wouldn't wake them up if they dozed in the swing or car, but I never put them on those places initially to go to sleep. I also kept them pretty active and moving during the times they were awake. Stimulation connects the ZZZs to reality: play in the sun and sleep with the moon. I also did not put them to sleep in a padded room either. My opinion is that if babies get used to only falling asleep in complete silence, that golden silence will come back to bite you in the end. 'Healthy noise' can be a lullaby too!"

(Gee, where was Margaret when I flubbed up on this point, turning on the attic fan from Day 1 to provide a cover of "white noise" for my baby's naps, and addicting them to "golden silence"? She's right. That white noise thing did come back to bite me in the end, as both my boys have turned into notoriously light sleepers.)

### Find the Magic Moment

Identify the magic moment when your child begins to nod off. "Kids can't just fall asleep like a lightbulb turning off," says Mindell. They wind down; they grow calmer. You can see it happening if you watch for it." Every baby is different, but many, including yours, could fall asleep as early as 7 or 8 P.M. "If you miss that window of opportunity, your overly tired child may grow agitated and cranky, and it'll be that much harder to get him to sleep."[3]

### No Entertainment

"Don't entertain him or you'll send the message that you're willing to be a playmate at 4 A.M.," says writer Linda Henry.[4] She's so right. Like Ann

 **Spit Up Happens**

Has your little one lost her "extrusion reflex," which makes her spit out everything but liquids? If so, and you think your little chow-hound is ready for something a little more chunky than formula or breast milk, try shoveling in a tiny spoonful of rice cereal and see what happens. (Rice cereal is the type least likely to trigger food allergies.) If Baby goes "blechhhh" and blows the goop all over you, don't worry. Her inborn iron stores won't need to be replenished until she's six months old.

(see "Voices" below), you've got to be somewhat businesslike in your nightly meetings with your baby. Though it's not likely you actually feel like playing. After all, weren't you in a wonderful dream set in Fiji just moments ago? Still, try to keep things dark and quiet. Baby will get the clue that the middle of the night is in fact not the time for Six Flags over Mommy. Daddy won't be sticking things up his nostrils to make him laugh, and that hilarious cat is nowhere to be seen. You know what they say about all work and no play? Yup, it makes for a dull boy, and a dull boy sleeps more readily than a highly amused one.

 **Voices**

"Adam (at four months) is still not sleeping through the night, although he is all business about night feedings. I keep the lights low, feed and change him, and put him right back to bed. Even if he is not asleep when I put him back in his crib, he will drop off soon. I'm very into Adam learning how to go to sleep on his own!"

—Ann

"We say our boys are not good sleepers, but maybe that's because we spoiled them. I nursed Bennett about one or two times a night until he was a year. I finally let him 'cry it out.' First I would let him cry for five minutes. Then I'd go in and talk to him a bit, settling him down, and I'd leave. He would cry some more, and I'd go back in ten minutes, go through the same routine, then fifteen minutes later, and so on, until he fell asleep. Two or three 'bedtimes' (nap or night) of that, and things were much better. If there is a next time and we have another baby, I hope I will have the guts to start [sleep training] sooner than a year old. We used this method with Max, too, except he was six months old when we started. Bennett just seemed so little and babyish longer. Max didn't sleep perfectly, though, until he was

## When Baby Can Make It Through the Night

After four months, apparently Baby can really, truly make it through the night with no food, much like you and me. If you want to make sure that a breast-fed infant doesn't really need that 3 A.M. meal, have your husband go in with a bottle when the baby cries. If he's not interested in eating and goes back to sleep, you'll know he's nursing primarily for comfort.

## Crying It Out

For crying out loud, it's time! This is it, the moment you've been dreading ever since you first realized it was a must: The time has come for you to let

in a bed and had a blanket that kept him covered all night and he had more space to toss and turn. So there is hope!"

—Alanna

"Amelia still does not sleep through the night, and she is approaching three years old. We tried every type of sleep training available including Ferber and Weissbluth but found that (a) it didn't work and (b) it was too hard on me to hear her cry like that. It just didn't feel right in my heart. A friend of mine put me in touch with a Dr. Jeffrey Hull in the States, and he was incredibly helpful. I also got hold of a book that is now out of print called *Sleepless Children: A Handbook for Parents* by a Dr. Haslam. It was also very helpful. What we have learned is that we should just relax and realize that we can't change Amelia. This is the way she is. If she cries it is for a reason, even if that reason is needing a hug. I won't tell her that needing a hug is not a valid enough reason for me to go to her when she cries. Now that she knows this, she is a lot more secure about staying in her bed by herself at night and she is not waking up as often."

—Laura

your precious infant "cry it out." Experts say that this process, also known as "Ferberizing" after the famous Dr. Ferber who pioneered this method, should wait until Baby is three months old and can soothe herself by sucking on her thumb, finger, or a pacifier.

Here's the drill: Follow your baby's normal bedtime routine. When she's sleepy, put her in her crib and leave the room. She'll probably put up a fuss. Leave for five to eight minutes and then go in and pat her, talk to her, and generally let her know she has not been left to the wolves, although she's howling like one (and you feel like the worst mother who ever lived). Repeat this process until Baby goes to sleep, adding about a minute to the time away from her crib each round. Most of the time, even the most stubborn baby caves in and sleeps after about forty-five minutes of good old-fashioned screaming her head off. You will feel tense when the baby wails—it's an innate mommy response. (Perhaps at your house it's the dad who can't hack the teary storms of his baby. I've heard stories from friends whose husbands have completely messed up their attempts to Ferberize by barging in and scooping up their wailing infant. You might want to discuss possible scenarios and strategies before that happens and try for a united front. If both of you aren't dedicated to making this work, it just won't.)

 **Quotable**

"Ninety percent of all infants sleep through the night—six to eight hours—by the age of three months, the American Academy of Pediatrics has reported."[5]

Some novice sleep trainers have gone to another part of the house or shut the door of their room to distance themselves from the noise. You could also sit on the toilet and run bath water, or listen to music on your headphones (see sidebar). Note: If your baby wakes up three hours later that night, don't start all over again when you're conked out yourself and

## To "Schedule" Baby or "Feed on Cue"?

### "Why I Chose the 'Scheduling Sleep' Method for My Baby"

"Is she sleeping through the night yet?" Yes, I explained, my six-month-old had been sleeping through the night for five months. Those sleepless nights were now a distant, foggy memory. Was it coincidence or my baby's nature that allowed her to sleep through the night so early? Or was it a purposeful "program" of scheduled feedings and sleep training?

After having my second baby sleep through the night at two months, it seems clear to me that scheduled feedings and sleep training really work. There are many people who support scheduled feedings to the point of gospel, but I don't. Scheduling is not a moral or biblical issue, but it is a choice!

Having said that, there are benefits to scheduling. One benefit is that Mom and Baby get longer and better quality sleep earlier. This allows Mom to be in a better mood and more able to handle life's stresses, including caring for a newborn baby. Also, the baby is happy because she gets good sleep. Babies are fussy and cry when they are tired; if they are well rested, they can take on the world! Another benefit is a predictable schedule that allows you to plan outings and other life events easily. The baby likes the security of a predictable schedule, too!

The method has three components: scheduled feedings, a feed-wake-sleep cycle, and sleep training. The important aspect of scheduled feedings is to not feed them whenever they cry. We learned to assess our babies' cries to determine the cause. Were they wet, tired, overstimulated? Did they need to burp? If we felt that they were hungry, we would feed them, even if it meant feeding them earlier than their scheduled time. It was very important to not allow them to fall asleep right after feeding and instead to put them on a feed-wake-sleep cycle. After some time awake, the baby is tired, and she learns to sleep because she is tired, not because her tummy is full. Sleep training is important because it prevents a baby from being dependent on external factors in order to sleep. Our babies learned to fall asleep on their own, without rocking, feeding, a car ride, or a vibrating bouncy seat. Sleep training necessitates listening to some crying before the baby falls asleep. We have listened to our share of crying, which was difficult, but the benefit of a happy baby is worth it!

I recently received an e-mail from a friend, who wrote, "Thanks for telling me about scheduling and sleep training—it really works!" I routinely recommend this to friends and, as a physician, sometimes to patients. Your personality has a lot to do with how successfully you will be able to implement the schedule. Scheduling definitely takes some investment, especially during the early days. We have done quite a bit of reading and cry analysis in our home. It is also good to remember that it takes awhile for the baby to catch on. If you are a persevering type of person, then this is for you. For weeks, it will seem like scheduling is not working, then one day it all clicks! The result will be people constantly commenting, "Your baby is so happy!"

—MEREDITH FURNESS, M.D., MOTHER OF LINDSAY AND BETHANY

### "Why I Decided to Feed on Cue"

Breast-feeding did not come naturally for my son and me. The first time I nursed him in the hospital he latched on, sucked once, and fell asleep. Our first week together was very rough; he lost a whole pound of his birth weight. The nurse who visited me in my home told me that I should nurse him as often as possible. Feeding him on cue helped us to form a good breast-feeding relationship. For the first year of his life he was always in the ninety-fifth percentile for height and the fiftieth percentile for weight. So it made perfect sense to feed him whenever he wanted to eat.

Everything I had read about breast-feeding emphasized how important it was to feed every two to three hours to establish your milk supply. Also, you should breast-feed at least eight to twelve times in a twenty-four-hour period. Babies' stomachs are the size of their tiny fist, and breast milk is digested quickly, so it makes sense that they need to eat often during the day and night. I think every breast-feeding mom worries, "Do I have enough milk?" One way to not worry is to feed whenever your baby is hungry or fussy.

Most of my friends fed on cue. My sister had two babies, whom she fed on cue, before my son was born. I saw what a close relationship she had with both of her toddlers. I think that is because she always responded to them when they cried. Also, I attended La Leche League meetings when I was pregnant and after my baby was born. The majority of moms who are LLL members feed on cue. Also, I have heard that most pediatricians encourage the "feed-on-cue" method. Mine certainly did!

The temperament of my baby influenced my decision to feed on cue. Feeding my baby whenever he was hungry or fussy just worked well for both of us. I don't know anyone who likes to listen to a baby cry. Most of the time I was able to comfort my son by breast-feeding him. Friends and acquaintances always commented about what a happy and content baby I had. Some wondered if he ever cried! Feeding him was the easiest way to get him to sleep for naps or for nighttime, it also was the easiest way to get him back to sleep when he woke in the middle of the night.

—Valerie Gee, accredited La Leche League Leader
and mom to Harold III and Baby-to-Be

your resolve is at a low ebb, to say the least. Pick it up tomorrow night, and hopefully things will get better. Repeat for four or five nights, maybe even a week or ten days. One of two things will happen: Either the munchkin will in fact get the hint and drop off to dreamland on a nightly basis, or you'll call the men in white to take you to the funny farm. Either way, you'll get more sleep.

# The Top Ten Things to Have in Your Medicine Chest

## 1. Thermometer
Ask your doctor to show you how to plug that thing in so you feel a little more confident. This mini-lesson will stand you in good stead at 3 A.M. one day, I promise you!

## 2. Infants' Nonaspirin Liquid Pain Reliever
You'll need a good pain and fever reducer (acetaminophen or ibuprofen) for the colds and fevers Baby is sure to get. And you don't want to have to run out in the middle of the night for meds, trust me!

## 3. A Pair of Safety Manicure Scissors
Oh joy! Isn't it fun to hold your breath and dive in to your baby's perfect little nails for a clipping session? We've all taken a chunk or two out of our baby's fingers—and cried—so you're not alone.

## 4. Baby-Safe Sunscreen Lotion

## 5. Baby-Safe Insect Repellent

## 6. Pediatrician-Approved Infant-Strength Liquid Decongestant

### 7. Nasal Aspirator Bulb Syringe

For what else? Sucking mucus out of a stuffy nose.

### 8. Sterilized Cotton Balls

These will help you clean the crusties out of eyes and noses.

### 9. Oral Syringe

Use the syringe to give meds such as antibiotics for ear infections.

### 10. Pedialyte

This good stuff replenishes fluids lost to diarrhea and other natural disasters. (Again, this is something you'll want to have on hand because babies typically are not overly concerned about the timing of their intestinal illnesses.)

## On the Relationship Seat: Your Pediatric Ally

I raved in the previous chapter about my pediatrician, Dr. Addy, but I know not all physicians are like her. There are other wonderful pediatricians out there, of course, and I hope you've been fortunate enough to have found one.

Regardless of whether your doctor is the cat's pajamas, there are several things you can do to keep your relationship with him or her strong—an important factor in those wee hours when you might be rousing him out of bed with a question about what the color of the mucus in your child's nose actually means. Your level of comfort with and confidence in your pediatrician will affect—consciously or not—the depth of care your child ultimately receives.

### Find Support

Of number-one importance is finding a physician who supports your parenting persuasions on topics such as feeding, sleeping, antibiotics, vaccines, and treatment options. If you feel railroaded by your doctor's opinions, stand respectfully firm. Find out all your options and listen carefully to the physician's recommendations. Then make your decision.

          **Quotable**

"There's nothing more exciting than interacting with your child, and one way to do that is through music, particularly before they can speak. Music is comforting and helps your children develop their imagination and sense of humor. It's also a wonderful way to teach them words—'Old McDonald had a what?' for example. Then, as they grow, they can either find music that is an expression of their life or they can make music that expresses their feelings. And you can never start too young. When they were babies, I sang to my children and held them as they went to sleep. I made up songs and sang traditional nursery rhymes. Anything works."

—Yo Yo Ma, cellist, father of Nicholas, 19, and Emily, 16

Most of the time, differences can be worked out. If not, you might need to find another physician. There's no point in spending valuable time going head-to-head on a regular basis with the very person who is your key partner in assuring your child's health.

### Getting to Know You

Get to know the staff members in your doctor's office. Learn their names and try to remember details about their work or personal lives as they present themselves. Chances are you'll spend more time over the course of your baby's childhood with the administrators, nurses, and physician's assistants than with the doctor. Their support of you is as important as your doctor's. If your pediatrician is in a group practice or clinic, you can usually make an appointment for a short interview with the other doctors at no charge. This get-to-know-you interview could prove helpful when your doctor has the night (or week) off and the on-call physician must oversee your emergencies.

## Take Charge

Be on top of your child's health by learning what might be affecting your child. Read the materials your pediatrician provides. Do your own research and ask your physician's opinions of what you find. Ask your doctor to recommend books, Web sites, or other materials that could help you learn more about specific health issues. Frustrated parents often give doctors a bad rap for not being able to pinpoint exact problems immediately and effectively. You can avoid this problem, win your doctor's respect, and, most important, aid your child's well-being by being a true partner.

## No Assumptions

Don't assume your doctor remembers everything about your child at each visit, especially if your child is generally healthy and only appears for routine checkups. Even the best doctors can lose track of details between visits, so take responsibility for reminding your doctor of key information—allergies, family health histories, visits to other specialists—as needed.

## Show Up on Time

Respect your doctor's time by showing up for appointments on time. When making the appointment, be as specific as you can about exactly what you need to discuss and/or what your child's symptoms are and how long they've been present. Write down your questions and concerns in advance so you can make the most of each appointment and avoid unnecessary follow-up calls. When calling about nonimmediate issues (in other words, your child doesn't need to be seen right away, or a delayed answer won't interrupt your child's well-being), call in the afternoons. Morning hours at most clinics are crazy, emergency-filled times, and staff appreciate those who keep the noncritical issues for the afternoon.

---

Mutual respect is at the heart of a good pediatrician-parent relationship. Expect your doctor to earn your respect, and do all you can to win hers as well.

Dear Jacob,

I can hardly believe how time has flown by since you were born just five months ago. Wasn't it just yesterday we were marveling at your little fingers, wondering how they would ever grow? And today your fingers are your constant entertainment! That little balled-up hand keeps going into your mouth any spare moment you get. You must be teething.

Your hair is finally growing a bit more, but you are still quite a baldy. Your eyes are dark blue, which makes me think they might change color yet to become beautiful browns like your daddy's. Today we blew bubbles, and you watched in wonder as every one of them tumbled down and popped (if our dog, Shelby, did not get them first). You love watching Shelby, and your eyes follow her everywhere you can hear her.

You love movement. Your swing and your stroller make you very content. We watch the birds from the window as I name them off—how exciting to see you marvel at all the new things! I can't wait to explain to you how nature works and to tell you all the names of the trees and birds, the clouds and flowers. I am really looking forward to seeing how you like the beach this summer with all the sand, water, and wind. Will you love the outdoors as much as Daddy and I do?

The best part of the day for me is your first smile of the morning, which usually comes right after I've fed you. Those little gums of yours make me laugh, and your eyes love to watch me. The second-best part of the day is when we hear you kick. You love to kick at night in bed as you are falling asleep, and Daddy and I lay in our bed giggling at the sounds you make. Maybe we should nickname you "Thumper."

It's been such a wonderful five months. I want time to stand still so I can remember you like this forever, but I know there is so much fun and adventure ahead. I look forward to making many memories with you and teaching you about how much Jesus loves you.

Love,

Mama

—Jessica Westra, mother of Jacob

# Colds, Constipation, and Your Cramped Love Life

*Milemarker!* C'mon, Baby, do the locomotion with me! Getting stronger and more active every day, your baby can get herself into all kinds of positions. She may even locomote by rocking, rolling, and twisting on her back, or by kicking against a flat surface. She rolls over easily now, so start babyproofing!

## Gesundheit, Baby!

What's up with your angel? Suddenly your little go-getter with the appetite of a horse and the energy of ten has slowed way down, more content to sit drowsily in your lap and stare at the walls than do anything else. "Ha-chooooo!" Baby sneezes, and his little chin is covered in mucus. Poor little guy!

 **Constipation**

Is your little one experiencing a jam session in his pipes? The culprit could be too much iron in his formula, but chat with your doctor before switching. To treat constipation, try giving your baby a little prune juice or corn syrup in her bottle or a teaspoon of healthy wheat germ in his rice cereal. Keep him well hydrated, too.

Your baby has his first cold, the premiere showing of the good old-fashioned sick flick that will play, reel to glassy-eyed reel, about eight to ten times before he's two. So get ready, Flo Nightingale, and put on your nurse's cap: It's show time! Here are some time-tested, baby-safe ways to make your little one as comfortable as possible.

### There She Blows!

Snot happens, and it's your job to keep Baby's nose clean and dry, even in a hurricane of mucous explosions. After a few dozen sneezes and drips, your angel's nose is bound is get red and sore. Spring for a box of those cushy, lotion-infused tissues for some extra TLC. Also, old-fashioned Vaseline or Bag Balm, with their timeless healing properties, soothe chapped nostrils and work like a charm to gently slough off the crusties the morning after a night of sniffling.

### Keep Baby Watered

With a runny nose and a fever, your wee sickie may not feel like eating or even drinking, which may lead to dehydration. Nurse more frequently or add an ounce or two to your baby's bottle, if she'll take it. If you still think she's not getting enough fluids, try a flavored electrolyte rehydration solution formulated for kids to help restore lost fluids. An excess of water can easily tip the balance of salts in Baby's body, and juice can cause diarrhea—the very last thing on the planet you need right now.

### "Better Parenting Through Drugs"

This is my pal Ann's cheeky little maxim for moments like these. Don't freak out! I simply mean employing use of pediatrician/FDA-sanctioned medications in appropriate dosages. I have heard many moms express distaste for "medicating" their children, but I have no such qualms. If a dropperful of baby decongestant will make my little guy feel more comfortable and less miserable, why not? (And by the way, there's no big prize—a trip to Maui, a new dining room set, $1,000—at the end of your child's babyhood for not ever administering a drop of acetaminophen. I checked.)

## Quotable

"The quality of your time together is extremely important, not just the quantity: If you find that you're a better parent when you work (whether it's because you reduce your family's financial stress or because you need the mental stimulation), then go ahead and do it. A parent who is happy and emotionally available is always better than one who is unhappy, frustrated, and distracted."[1]

—Anita Sethi, Ph.D.

Confirm with your pediatrician before giving your baby any cold or cough medicines. Given with care, decongestants may bring much-needed relief to a fussy mommy—er, baby.

### Suck Up the Gunk

You and your baby will not be on speaking terms after this next trick, so I apologize up front. Sometimes you just gotta go in where angels fear to tread—your baby's nostrils—and suck out the gunk that's been causing all the trouble. Yup, it may be time to whip up a watery batch of saline solution and demucus your baby's nose. Mix one-quarter teaspoon of salt with eight ounces of water, slurp up a few drops with a bulb syringe or dropper, and give two or three squirts up each nostril. Then wait a minute to let the drops dissolve the mucus and go back in again, this time to Roto-Rooter out the snot. Ezra loathed this little home remedy—can you blame him?—though it did alleviate his suffering for a little while. Not that he knew that.

There are some less traumatic ways to fight congestion:

## A Good Steam Bath

Put Baby in his car seat or sit with him on your lap while you run a hot shower and let steam fill the room. (Or, as one mom discovered, do the opposite and bring your bundled, stuffy baby into the cold, dry winter air. This particular little snuffle-up-a-Gus cleared right up!)

## Napping Upright

Let him nap in his front carrier while you walk around. The upright angle will clear congestion, and he'll be soothed snuggling close to your warm form. Depending on his age, you might want to try having him sleep all night or nap in his car seat. The elevation will help him get some much-needed ZZZs.

## Humidifier

Place a cool-mist humidifier in his room while he sleeps.

## Don't Push Foods

Your baby probably won't be hungry so don't push food. Cool, sweet foods, such as applesauce, or bland foods, such as pastas and toast, have the best chance of actually getting down the hatch. If you've been cooped up for a couple of days, a stroll outside in the fresh air may do both of you a world of good, unless it's thirty below or baby has a high temperature.

## Bond with Baby

Finally, remember that your baby will get better, and his baby illnesses are actually times of bonding, brief windows of time where the two of you can snuggle in together, hibernating with your honey until the storm of sickness blows over.

Take it from Dr. William Sears, the Dr. Spock of our day: "While infant illnesses cause babies to lose sleep and parents to miss work, it helps to view them as opportunities to connect with your baby," he says. "Infants naturally become clingy when ill, so take advantage of the extra cuddle time. In addition to the treatments above, they need the tender loving care that only Mom and Dad can provide."[2]

## On the Relationship Seat: Your Main Man

Remember him, the guy who got you into this in the first place? No relationship is more drastically metamorphosed by children than that between you and your husband. As of December 6, 1997, I ceased to become solely Lori, Doyle's wife, the one who used to go fishing in the dark with him, who poured coffee on her pancakes one foggy morning on our honeymoon, and who would stay up late to watch Conan O'Brien with my second-shifter mate. When the nurse handed me that wrapped and squalling bundle, the bulk of my time, energy, and attention shifted to Jonah.

I had read rapturous statements and heard glowing, firsthand accounts of people for whom parenthood was the ultimate romance booster, aphrodisiac, and "perfect breeding ground for our love," as one gushy acquaintance of mine slobbered about his wife and their new-parent status. (Gee, how far back in one's head *can* one's eyes roll?)

Certainly, it does make you regard your husband in a new way, as your baby's papa, which tightens the knot of your union that much more securely. After all, more is at stake now: your precious baby's well-being! She needs a mom and a dad for the optimum good life, experts say, and you know they are right. You see your guy's smile in your baby's face, his calm spirit, your mother-in-law's hair color on her sweet tiny tresses. It's enough to give you a humbling sense of the profound ways you and your husband are linked. If your baby is adopted, as I was, you may not see physical resemblances, at least not yet—those will come in the miracle of adoption—but you are overwhelmed with the enormous sense of shared responsibility. In many ways, a baby is a bonding agent of her parents' love and commitment to each other.

The flip side of this is that you will have to work double-time and triple-time to nourish your relationship, to uphold your vows to love, honor, and cherish. This isn't easy. I once heard that, with every baby born into a family, the husband and wife find themselves that much further apart and have to exert that much more effort to find their way back to each other. Wait a sec, Lorilee, didn't you just say babies are the uber-glue of marriage, the flypaper of fondness, adhesive of ardor? (I could go on but obviously have become carried away. My apologies. Keep reading if you will.)

Ahem. Yes! I did say something to that effect, but in my opinion, marriage also becomes quite a bit harder.

"The three that Baby makes isn't necessarily a crowd, but he can crowd your days and nights so much that you have no time left for the company of two," the authors of *What to Expect the First Year* write. "The period of new parenthood is actually one during which it is very easy for couples to grow apart instead of closer."[3]

Remember your first date, when your husband-to-be cleaned up real good and wore a big smile, a twinkle in his eye, and some sort of yummy smelling cologne? Now his face is scratchy, his eyes are fogged over, and—

**Parenting on the Web:
A List of Must-Surf Sites**

- American Academy of Pediatrics: www.aap.org
- Consumer Product Safety Commission: www.cpsc.gov
- La Leche League International: www.lalecheleague.org
- www.babycenter.com (my favorite!)
- www.babystyle.com (cute stuff!)

what is that smell? Eau de Baby Urp is his scent of the moment. You're both more tired than you ever thought possible. Experts say that new parents lose between 400 and 750 hours of sleep the first year of Baby's life—which is making you both cranky and short-tempered. Sex? We'll get to that in a minute, but that whole realm is operating at an all-time low ebb. In fact, prisoners with conjugal visits are getting more action than you two. Last night might have been a good time to get busy between the sheets, except that Baby's presence in the bassinet ten inches from your bed gave you the willies, and you got into a fight about the family bed issue—again.

It's easy to let your marriage slide, to wake up one morning and suddenly regard your husband—the dude who used to make your palms sweat and your stomach flutter—as nothing more than a sperm donor/roommate. Don't let it happen. Just don't. Your connection with your husband is the very foundation upon which your new little family is built, and you know what the Good Book says about shifting sand.

Marriage counselors place all wed duos in two categories: (a) The Couple-Centered Marriage, and (b) The Child-Centered Marriage. Don't we all know pairs who barely have anything to say to each other anymore, who hover around their babies as if leaving them for a moment would result in catastrophe, who never go out alone together, like ever? They would fall into the *B* category, The Child-Centered Marriage. Other couples have found balance in their lives, carving out blocks of time and finding energy to fan the flame of their love while still caring well for their children's needs.

## YOUR RELATIONSHIP WITH YOUR HUSBAND IS MORE IMPORTANT THAN YOUR RELATIONSHIP WITH YOUR BABY.

No joke. You simply must exert some serious attention to your love life, or your entire family could be in jeopardy. And I'm not being melodramatic here. I've seen families dissolve in divorce court because one or both partners have sorely neglected their couplehood, all in the name of being devoted parents. The best thing you can do for your baby, besides staying close to your heavenly Father, is to stake your tent in Camp A: The Couple-Centered Marriage. Take showers together. Hang out on the couch after Baby's asleep. Be mindful of your partner, asking him how his day went and how many fish—and what kind—he and the guys caught on their fishing trip. Make a conscious effort not to talk about the baby for fifteen minutes a day. Go out together and leave Baby with your mother, the in-laws, or a reliable baby-sitter. My word! Baby will be just fine without you for a couple of hours, but if you neglect your marriage, he'll be anything but fine in the long run.

## Sex: What a Concept!

"And speaking of sex: Since you'll be thin and childbirth will have been pain-free and Baby will sleep on demand, sex will once again be fabulous. You don't know whether you'll even be able to wait six weeks!"[4]

Yeah, she's joking, "she" being writer Pamela Redmond Satran, capping off her funny list of ten pregnancy fantasies. Great sex soon after Baby's arrival is in fact a fantasy that rivals a sitcom-style labor and going home from the hospital in your pre-baby jeans. You don't often hear about post-childbirth women who are just rarin' to go, who simply cannot wait to do the mattress mambo with Loverboy. Usually you hear whispers like, "It hurt like crazy" or "I finally told him that my doctor didn't think sex was a good idea for, like, months after the baby was born." Engaging in nookie for the first time after you've become parents is akin to engaging in nookie for the first time ever.

Plus, now the whole idea sounds about as appealing as falling out of an airplane—for you, anyway. But since your Maker knows your post-partum season shouldn't become another prenatal one, He's designed your body with some inborn birth-control functions. Number one, since

**Voices**

"I had a VBAC [vaginal birth after cesarean] with our second child, so I wasn't sure what to expect with the episiotomy thing. The first time, even though I had waited until the episiotomy had healed, it hurt like CRAZY! I cried and had to take pain medication. It got easier after that first time, and by the third time I felt no pain at all."

—Dale

"I didn't know it then, but I had terrible rectal tears from giving birth to Maiya. I saw my doctor at the six-week appointment, and right before he checked me, he said, 'This (examination) is going to really hurt,' so I know he could see how bad it was. Too bad he didn't warn me [about intercourse]. The first time my husband and I had sex, it was awful. I swore off it for life! It was about six months before I could enjoy sex again."

—Katie

"Once we picked a free night, I cut back on Alicia's nap so she would go to bed earlier—and easier. We turned our bedroom into a hot date spot: candles, music, munchies, hot apple cider. We timed it for the best chance of our baby not waking up in the middle of everything. We relaxed by reading for a while, then we gave each other back rubs, and then...well, things got more interesting! I almost fell asleep after my back rub, so I had to kind of snap out of it so I could give him one too. (If I'd fallen asleep, he would have been seriously bummed!) We only did this super-planned thing once, but I would do it again next time we have a baby. I felt pretty relaxed and so did my husband, and it worked wonders for our love life!"

—Emma

your placenta is gone—and that used to produce estrogen in place of your ovaries—your desire-producing hormones are on leave, from a month to a year if you're breast-feeding exclusively. Once your ovaries kick in again, you may warm up to the idea of sex. Throw in possible PPD, fatigue, and body image issues, and your libido may be out to lunch for some time. So what's up with the ixnay on intercourse? Here are a few likely culprits.

## The Top Ten Postpartum Lust Busters

1. You feel about as sexual as a commercial for Preparation H.
2. The *H* in Preparation H—not exactly a big turnon.
3. You look down at your saggy breasts, your Jell-O tummy, those purple stripes zigzagging over your thighs, and you think to yourself, "The old gray mare, she ain't what she used to be."
4. Your breasts have been co-opted by a fifteen-pound man— your baby.
5. If it's a choice between sleep and sex? Well, duh!
6. Your husband—FATHER OF THE CHILD YOU SO KINDLY GAVE BIRTH TO AFTER FIFTY-ONE HOURS OF MIND-BENDING PAIN—said he was too tired to look after Baby while you went out for coffee with your girlfriend.
7. You're too tired to look after Baby while he goes golfing.
8. You don't even have time for a shower half the time, never mind foreplay.
9. One word: *episiotomy.*
10. Your child is in the same bed as you, like, right there, and you're supposed to copulate?

At this point, your husband probably wouldn't care if Baby were still snoozing in the family bed. (But let's face it, he probably wouldn't mind if his entire extended family were in the bedroom with you, present and accounted for, including his large cousin, Big Hilda.) You, however, are a different story. Sex used to be rather entertaining, but since you pushed

Baby Waldo—all eleven pounds, three ounces of him—into this world, it just doesn't hold the same appeal. Hopefully your husband is patient and sensitive. Remind him gently yet firmly that sex does indeed start in the kitchen or at the changing table, as it were. Many women experience resentment over having to do the lion's share of the housework and baby care, and resentment isn't exactly a big desire-booster. Talk openly about your expectations of labor division, not to mention your gut-feelings about your evolving sexuality. Stock up on KY, try to grab a nap once in a while, and keep a sense of humor about the whole thing. My friend Ann offers the following advice on postpartum sex: "Two words: baby swing," she says, with characteristic frankness. "Get the kind with batteries, though. You don't want to have to keep jumping out of bed to wind the thing up. Still, after our first baby was born, we discovered that sex can happen in the exact time it takes for the baby swing to wind down."

You will feel randy again, if not tomorrow then by the time Waldo is old enough to ride a bike. And don't worry about your new love handles. According to author Debra Waterhouse, your guy couldn't care less: "Your husband's probably dying to see your naked body, and would die and go to heaven if you initiated sex and abandoned yourself in the act with full body acceptance," she writes. "Just ask him."⁵

Dear Adam,

A new adventure began as we opened up your first box of baby cereal.

At first, you weren't so sure about what we were trying to feed you. *This is not how food is supposed to be*, you must have thought. We'd put the spoonful of cereal into your mouth, and out it would come again as you gave us a look of bewildered disgust. But rejection quickly gave way to curiosity, then acceptance. Now you eagerly lean forward in your high chair, mouth open wide, ready to gobble up whatever is on your spoon.

Through it all you were determined to learn this new experience hands-on. You didn't just want to be fed; you wanted to investigate the spoon. We let you do this once and had to clean barley out of your eyebrows as a result. For a while you liked to grab the cereal off the spoon and attempt to finger-paint your forehead with it. Last week you learned what happens when you make your favorite new buzzing sound with your cheeks full of oatmeal. Feeding you is messy business, and you've taught your two perfectionist parents to let go of our preconceived opinions of what "should be" and just enjoy "what is."

Our solid food experience has also given us precious early glimpses of who you are as a person. God created you with your own unique personality and talents, and one of our greatest joys as your parents will be to watch these characteristics unfold and to help you grow in them and use them to serve God and other people. As we nourish your body with food in your infancy, we pray that God will nourish your soul through us, put a deep love for Jesus in your heart, and fill you with wisdom and faith in the years ahead.

Love,

Mom and Dad

—Dan and Ann Baker, parents of Adam

# Amigos, Amoxicillin, and Amazing Reads

*Milemarker!* Right about now you can expect to see Baby's two front teeth. Next up: Watch for her two lateral incisors. Don't be alarmed if your baby has gaps between some of her pearly whites. Teeth often come through the gums at odd angles, and any spaces commonly disappear after all twenty baby teeth have emerged. Once your baby starts teething, you can expect more drooling and experimenting with sounds as she adjusts to having these bizarre new things in her mouth. Cold, wet washcloths, icy teething rings, and topical pain remedies such as Baby Orajel help soothe the ouch.

## On the Relationship Seat: The Buddy System

My buddies Rachel and Mary Jo and I have had some amazing girlfriends' getaways over the years. There was that time in Chicago, on New Year's Eve, when we ate at this swanky restaurant—lobster ravioli, warm duck salad with walnuts and Gorgonzola… You get the picture. We figured this decadence would set us back about thirty dollars a person, at the most. Well, golly gee, were our faces red when we got the bill and it ran into triple digits—per person. (That the menu had no prices should have been our first clue.) This was before I had my first baby, Jonah. *Après* Baby, a weekender with pals became an undertaking of massive proportions. We did swing a day trip to Ann Arbor last summer, where we bookwormed our way through about twelve used bookstores. Plus, I very much enjoyed eating at a restaurant where chicken nuggets and hot dogs weren't on the menu. But now Mary Jo has Baby Josephine, and I have a preschooler and a toddler. Rachel, currently single (and honorary aunt to Jo Jo, Ez, and Feeny), could take off and do the weekends and day trips by herself if she wanted, but what fun would that be?

Sigh. Life sure has changed since the three of us could go to chick flicks on the spur of the moment, leisurely sip our lattes and chat up new and fabulous reads, and shop for open-toed sandals in a size seven ladies. We're all at slightly different places on the continuum of life, which means it's become more and more of a challenge to stay connected.

"Your friendships undergo dramatic transformations," says writer Paula Spencer. "That's because the kind of support and socializing you need evolves along with your baby, as does the amount of free time you have and how you want to spend it."[1] Still, even though new moms are wrapped up in a world of Diaper Genies and late-breaking colic news, we need our amigos more than ever.

My husband likes to say that my friends are my hobbies, and he's dead-on. One of the things I am most proud of in this world is the fact that I still keep in touch with all ten of my bridesmaids. Yes, ten. It was a bit much, as wedding guests got whiplash craning their necks to see each new velvet-garbed girl make her way down the aisle. But I wouldn't change a thing, even if my mother would. It hasn't been effortless to maintain these relationships, and in fact with one or two of these girls, the link loosens up year by year. But I've learned volumes about the art and craft of nurturing friendships.

You already know this: Baby has reshaped your relationships with your chums. You will win some, and lose some, and grow closer to others, and that's the truth. Here's my two cents on finding and keeping good, call-'em-at-3-A.M. pals in this new season of life.

## Singles

Remember when you and your best friend camped out at the arena box office so you could get front row seats at the U2 concert? Now you're too tired to even listen to their latest CD—do they have a lullaby album, by the way?—and you sure didn't follow through with your pledge to name your firstborn Bono. Eddie Junior takes up most of your time, and that's as it should be. Your old head-banging crony? She loves Baby Ed as if he were her own nephew, but she wishes you could pry yourself away from him long enough to hear about her date with that drummer.

Friendships with singles can be the hardest to maintain, but I remain a huge fan. I wouldn't trade my sisterhood with Rachel, Sue, or Stephanie for a diaper-service truckload of bottle-wielding, tip-spouting mommy mates.

"Longtime friends have a history that's defined by more than one's breast-feeding status. The trick to keeping up is for both sides to make a concerted effort—and have lots of patience with each other," says Spencer.[2] So true, and plus, it can be refreshing to hear a different tune once in a while, a suddenly exotic piece of info from Planet Infantless about boyfriends and blind dates and job promotions.

 **Grace Words That Build Up Your Girlfriends**

- "I'm so proud of you."
- "I'm honored you would open up to me about this."
- "Congratulations on your new house/dog/niece/promotion/pregnancy!"
- "I prayed for you."
- "I'm so sorry. Poor you."
- "How can I help you through this?"
- "How's the baby/toddler/child/husband/dog?"

Seriously, don't ditch your kidless confidantes—it's a bad move. But keeping them will take some elbow grease on your end. Writer and single Camerin Courtney described her experience of being left out of the Clique of Motherhood. But she also had raves for one parent pal who reached out to her and forged a lasting bond: "In contrast, whenever Cindy, a married work contact and friend, and I run into each other at our local coffee shop, we chat about everything under the sun. I ask about her husband and two kids, especially about her eldest son who just started driving! And she asks about my pet parakeet, Mr. Right, and my latest travel plans. I love that this married woman acknowledges the things in my life (as opposed to the 'missing' ingredients of a spouse and/or kids), and that she values me by asking about these other interests, people, and hobbies."[3]

That's the key right there: Show your solo friends that they still matter. Remember their birthdays, ask about the date with the drummer, sympathize if they've had a hideous breakup, return their calls and e-mails. Variety is the spice of life, and sustaining relationships with friends who may not have tons in common with you anymore is, in the end, a stretching, positive thing. "If you want variety in your circle of friends, don't forget the single women in your neighborhood, workplace, and church group," Courtney writes. "You'll enrich each other's lives with your diverse perspectives and experiences for years to come."[4]

## Married Without Kids

"Kerby achieved the pincer grasp!" you exclaim in your breathless phone call to your best couple friends, updating them on the Kerb's latest developmental milestone. Thing is, they don't really care, even if they do know what a pincer grasp is. I mean, they might care, some, but truly, uppermost in their minds is when you and your husband are going to be ready to drop the baby off at your mom's—who lives next door—and go check out that new Italian restaurant that opened up months ago, when you were in labor, actually. DINKS (Double Income, No Kids) are much like the singles in your sphere. They think it's great that you were blessed with a baby, but they also feel some bewilderment as to the drastic changes in *their* social life because of *your* baby. No more drop-of-the-hat weekends to Cedar Point or impromptu dinner-and-a-movie nights. Watching a video at their place is pretty much out of the question now, and even trying to view one in your living room is getting tricky: "Shhh... Mute the TV... Was that the baby?" Plus, now you and your mate are way too tired to stay up past 9 P.M., which throws a wrench into things.

Your kinship with the doubles in your life could go south, and fast, unless you take action to stop the slide. Try to keep the baby news bulletins to a dull roar and remember that they have lives too, even if there's no child at the center of their orbit yet. Keep up your end of the dance by having them over for cookouts or, if you're not ready to relinquish 100 percent monitoring of Baby yet (and you should start getting ready for that about now), maybe you and your husband could swap one-on-one social encounters with one half of their unit. Don't be too jealous if they find new Best Couple Friends. Think of it as a wake-up call to try harder to maintain their friendship.

Your married-without-kids pals fall into two categories: Babies Someday and Babies Not Ever.

*The Babies Someday.* Does your married friend perceive your new baby as a gift to you or a prize awarded for beating her in the baby race? Tune in to how she feels about your new tyke and let that guide your adjusted friendship as it can. Does she want to become Baby's "Auntie"? Or does too much time with or talk about your child turn bittersweet, reminding her of what she doesn't have yet? Would your friendship with the couple be bolstered by get-togethers sans Baby, or would they be disappointed to leave the little guy out? Look for ways to balance your new family's needs (definitely a top priority!) with sensitivity to your friends' feelings about Baby and their own efforts to conceive.

*The Babies Not Ever.* I have some experience with this category, as my matron-of-honor, Carla, and her husband, Bryan, are childless by choice. What would you ever have to share with people who have voluntarily decided to forgo something you feel is the most important element of life itself? That's a good question, but truly, you probably still do have much in common. What brought you together in the first place? Not babies,

 **Voices**

"My friend, we'll call her Sue, and I were the kind of friends who talked daily about everything, had the same hobbies, and worked the same shift (often the third...and those who have worked this shift know the tongue automatically loosens after 2:30 A.M.). We pretty much knew everything about each other.

"One of our hobbies was going to garage sales together. Among the loads of 'treasures' we found, we also started to accumulate items for an eventual baby we would each have. (This started even before we were married.) As life progressed, we both got married, settled down, and began to think about having children. But there was one problem: Sue's husband decided he did not want to have children. That wasn't part of our plan! Sue felt terrible about it and decided not to push the issue. She figured her husband would come around.

"Meanwhile, I got pregnant. I was elated, but when I thought about telling Sue, I felt physically sick. When I went to tell her, she tried to be happy for me, but I know it was very hard for her. During the pregnancy, I found that when people asked me about how I was doing, I would tell the truth. But with Sue, I tried to make sure that the subject did not come up, and when it did, I would quickly tell her how awful it was and change the subject. My reasoning was that if I made pregnancy sound miserable enough, she would be relieved not to be pregnant. I continued this strange behavior even that's for sure. But there's always your faith journey, music, books, a similar wacky sense of humor, a shared history, or being fans of the same now defunct hockey team (go, Jets!).

In this case, be sure to keep baby stories to a minimum, especially the minutiae. Carla is interested in the big stuff with my kids, and your baby-less chum probably is too. I've noticed members of this group are usually not averse to children in general; they've just decided that's not something

after my son was born. I was elated at being a mother, but if I talked about it at all, I only told her about the parts of parenting that were no fun—'I'm a human milk-machine... He wakes up all the time at night... He cried for an hour and a half this morning.' Our daily phone conversations that once lasted an hour or more were no longer realistic, and I didn't have the same desire to be in touch with what was going on at the office.

"Things between us changed a lot and never really returned to where they were. Sue and her husband eventually divorced. I reduced my hours and responsibilities at work so that I could be at home more with my kids, while Sue got a promotion and became consumed with her job. We now talk once or twice a week. We try to console ourselves that we are still as close, just busier than we used to be. Maybe that's the case, maybe not. I've learned that God shows you through life events how He is in control of the plan, not you. My plan would have included play dates with Sue and her kids, stories about potty training, skinned knees, and sharing ways in which our kids show us how much they love us, but I guess God had something different in mind for both of us. Truthfully, though, it is sometimes hard for both of us to accept the change in our friendship."

—Sheri

for them. In fact, Carla and Bryan are a keen aunt and uncle to their nieces and nephews, plus they enjoy their friends' kiddies—in moderation. Above all, don't patronize your friends with the "Oh, you'll change your mind and have a baby someday" comment. You may secretly hope they will, but to express it on a regular basis? Zip your lips, or kiss that friendship good-bye.

## Triples, Quadruples, Quintuples (Cronies with One, Two, or Three Munchkins)

"A child is just the thing to nudge you onto the path of true friendship," says Spencer. "Parenthood is the ultimate common ground."[5]

Since you are admittedly obsessed with your baby, it is kinda cool to pal around with people who are currently on the same page. My friend Jane had Avery a month after I had Jonah; then, three years later, she gave birth to Ellie a mere twelve days into Ezra's life. When her husband, Jamie, rang on New Year's Day with the news that they had a new daughter, he said, "I guess we'll plan on a double wedding." It's been fun to trade anecdotes on the growth and development of our babies as they smile, roll over, crawl, and coo on parallel tracks. Jane knows I won't be yawning over her description of Ellie's first words, and I am comfortable relating in detail my struggles getting Ezra to sleep at night. Certainly, having babies at practically the same moments has bonded our families in a way we might not have been otherwise. Avery and Jonah hit it off as playmates, and hopefully Ez and Ellie will do the same. Jane and Jamie used to be our downtown-suppers-out friends, but now we sit in their basement playroom and are still able to complete our sentences because our four kids are in their own little world of play. We don't have to worry that Ezra will destroy some priceless souvenir from Fiji because (a) Jane and Jamie ain't going to Fiji anytime soon and (b) their house is totally childproofed.

As fun as it is to ride the same wave with the baby-toting gang, beware for that big spoiler: competition. "Oh, you say wee Moe is small for his age? Well, that's a shame. My Archie is off the charts for weight and height," Little Miss Ain't-We-Grand confides smugly. Ouch! We new parents are so gaga over our babies, and so wholly devoted to their well-being, that even the remotest sign that another child may be advanced nips at our sense of security and makes the mother bear in us roar in defensive protest. "These days, I can recognize competitive mothering at twenty paces, but there was a time when one snarky little remark could reduce me to a puddle of insecure tears," admits writer Vicki Iovine. "I was such easy prey, because I believed deep down I was faking my way through motherhood. Clearly, not only were these mothers far better than I was at childrearing, but their children were superior to mine too."[6]

Take any comments with a grain of salt, because sometimes mommy arrogance masks a deeper hurt or social cluelessness. I mean, we all think our babies are the most beautiful and brilliant, but we don't voice these things to people (except maybe to our family and best friends, who agree with us). I recently heard two different moms blathering on about how "advanced" their kids were, how little Yvonne and May would suffer so

 **Bosom E-Buddies**

The Internet is crammed with chat rooms and bulletin boards for new parents to get together to rant about their in-laws and HMOs or to rave about their babies. The best tips are always from other in-the-trenches moms and dads, and thousands of them generously give advice on the Web. Join a breast-feeding support group online (try www.lalecheleague.org), or meet a new mom who's also trying to juggle career and family (visit a bulletin board at www.parentsplace.com or www.parentsoup.com). Check out some of the other Web sites listed in "Parenting on the Web" in Month Five. Many fast and firm friendships have started this way, and at the very least you can get some great, reality-tested hints.

because they would be so far ahead of their classmates by the time pre-school rolled around. After I had time alone to roll my eyes a few times, it dawned on me that neither of these women had many friends, in no small part because they often make such social faux pas.

If a pal of yours is driving you nuts with her constant comparisons, you have a few choices. If she's just an acquaintance or a "fringe friend"—that is, not one of your core soul mates—blow it off. Life's too short to have a cow over an insensitive statement. But if the friend's competitive remarks are making you feel like a rival instead of a friend, it's time to tact-fully confront her: "When you say things like that, it makes me feel kind of hurt. I mean, all babies do things on their own timetable, so can't we just enjoy our kids and leave it at that?" She may be shocked or, worse, come back with a "my, aren't you oversensitive" comment. Take a deep breath and try to let the dust settle. Give yourself a little room to evaluate your friendship. It may not survive, but at least you've expressed yourself honestly and graciously. Try to stick close to chums who love, are full of grace and humor, and make your mothering journey an even richer experience.

## The Top Ten Books for Ma and Pa

1. *What to Expect the First Year* by Arlene Eisenberg, Heidi E. Murkoff, Sandee E. Hathaway
2. *Touchpoints: The Essential Reference: Your Child's Emotional and Behavioral Development* by T. Berry Brazelton, M.D.
3. *97 Ways to Make a Baby Laugh* by Jack Moore
4. *Bargain Buys for Baby's First Year* by Leah Severson
5. *Outsmarting the Female Fat Cell—After Pregnancy* by Debra Waterhouse
6. *Praying the Bible for Your Baby* by Heather Harpham Kopp
7. *So That's What They're For: Breastfeeding Basics* by Janet Tamaro
8. *Complete Book of Baby and Child Care* by Focus on the Family

9. *The Happiest Baby on the Block: The New Way to Calm Crying and Help Your Baby Sleep Longer* by Harvey Karp, M.D.
10. *The Baby Book: Everything You Need to Know About Your Baby from Birth to Age Two* by William Sears, M.D., and Martha Sears

## Blame It on the (Otitis) Media

Few things thrown at you the first year of parenting can cause you to become more unhinged than Baby's first ear infection. Not only is it difficult to witness your angel in pain, but ear infections can also mess up Baby's sleep and yours—and in fact the entire household's. Ain't nobody happy when Baby's got an earache. I'm telling you, the family goldfish won't be getting a good night's sleep until this thing is licked.

At the onset of your first infection, you will also be plunged into the fray of one of parenting's "hot buttons": How do you make it go away? Your sister-in-law bellows about the evils of antibiotics, and your neighbor brays about how some kid she knows lost hearing in one ear because his parents went the homeopathic route. Anyone over fifty is horrified you would even consider opting for a natural remedy, and everyone else is split into two camps:

- *Antibiotics Are Awesome.* They work, usually, and are safe, reliable, and doctor-condoned.
- *Antibiotics Are Awful.* They will only cause current strains of bacteria to be unresponsive, resulting in more medicine for less results. They are a tool of the medical industry, making doctors and pharmaceutical companies richer. In short, antibiotics are pretty much the root of all evil.

I'll just tell you up front that I fall into the first camp; I'm not much of a maverick when it comes to doctor's suggestions. Hey, what do I know that they don't? Not much. On the other hand, about half of all ear infections resolve themselves without antibiotics.[7]

I've had to cope with much more in the way of ear infections with my secondborn. Jonah had two ear infections his first two years of life and has since ceased having them. Ezra, on the other hand, has experienced more than his fair share of excruciating pain, sleepless nights, and down-the-hatch-whether-you-like-it-or-not episodes of antibiotics. He's amenable to the pink stuff (amoxicillin) which is wonderful, because who wants to attempt zapping that neon hue out of baby clothing (and grown-up clothing)? Not *moi*, I'll tell you that much.

Of course, after a few rounds of pink, we all know what comes next: the white stuff—Augmentin, which is supposed to blitzkrieg the most stubborn of bacteria out of Baby's system. If Ezra is any indication, babies look askance at the stronger medicine. I haven't tasted it, but I suspect, judging by my baby's rather violent aversion to it, that it's not a pleasant experience to swill it around one's mouth. But it must be imbibed, twice a day for ten days, or of course the little germies will enact a hostile takeover of the entire ear region. This means that the process of administering the medicine is kind of like force-feeding a thrashing twenty-pound crocodile. It's not pretty.

Assuming most of the vile liquid makes it down the esophagus—which is a fairly big assumption—all you can do at that point is pray you won't see it again, projecting out of Baby's mouth. It says right there on the label "Take with food," which is all well and good as long as Baby doesn't also have some kind of nasty cold/flu/virus thing that makes eating the last thing in the world he wants to do. Then it's up to Mom and Dad to figure out a way to get food—crackers, cereal, toast, anything edible—into a child who will likely regurgitate it within the hour. In this tricky maneuver, timing becomes key to the success of the entire operation. If you're not completely exhausted from cajoling your heart out to get the little sickie to eat something, you will be wiped out completely after then prying his mouth open and forcing the white stuff down. You see, this must be accomplished during the short window of opportunity while the food is still buffering his delicate tummy, not decorating your shirt.

I tell you, this sad scenario is enough to try the patience of a top-level diplomat and more than enough to prompt the staunchest fan of antibiotics to think holistic. A cursory glance at the Web will reveal all kinds of alternative treatments: massage, the chiropractor, echinacea drops, oils of olive and garlic. I myself tried to go the garlic oil route one time. Who knows if it helped, although a lady down the street (mother of seven) told me that the stuff has antibiotic properties and, when warmed, soothes the throbbing ear canal. So there I was, kneeling by the bathtub, puncturing capsules of garlic oil, which oozed into Ezra's ear. Compared to forcing the white stuff on him, the ear route seemed blissfully low-fuss. He did kind of look at me like, "Umm, Mom, what in the world are you doing this time?" And, it must be said, he stank to high heaven of garlic. For days the kid smelled up the joint something powerful until the garlicky scent faded into a rather nice Italian restaurant–type aroma. This made us all crave manicotti. But hey, it can't hurt, right?

On the prowl for ear-infection-fighting tips, I came across savvy info from online moms, who recommended everything from homeopathic remedies to aggressive prevention strategies, such as reducing dairy products in their children's diets, adjusting crib mattresses so their children

 **Ear Infections May Run in the Family**

Is your baby prone to ear infections? They could be hereditary, according to a study published in the January 1999 issue of the *Journal of the American Medical Association*.

While studying the incidence of ear infections in twins and triplets, doctors at the Otitis Media Research Center at the Children's Hospital of Pittsburgh made a surprising discovery. The chance that one sibling in an identical set would have an ear infection at some point after his sibling did was about 60 percent. With fraternal siblings, the chance was about 30 percent.

could sleep on an incline, and making use of humidifiers at the first sign of illness.

One Web posting caught my eye, this one from a mom named Lisa, who was truly perplexed about what to do for her daughter's ear troubles:

> My oldest child has never had an ear infection, and neither has my husband or I. My youngest daughter, who was exclusively breast-fed for seven months, got her first ear infection at two-and-a-half months. She has had seven ear infections in twelve-and-a-half months. She uses a pacifier only while she sleeps and does not drink out of bottles. We have tried four different antibiotics, and while they do get rid of the infections, three to four weeks later she has another one. She is not in daycare, and no one in the family smokes. I am at my wit's end. If anyone has had some good response with alternative treatments, please e-mail me.

Well, I did e-mail Lisa. True, I was about three years late, but about three minutes after I shot off the e-mail, my mailbox contained a reply from this Southern California mom, who had eventually found a solution to her baby's infection woes. Lisa wrote:

> My daughter is now four and a half, and she hasn't had an ear infection (knock, knock) in almost three years. We did osteopathic treatments and removed all dairy from her diet and all dust collec-tors (stuffed animals mostly) from her room. Within six months, the ear infections had stopped and she has not had a recurrence since, although she has been back on dairy since she was two and a half. We didn't even have to get rid of the binky! This treatment route was made after we saw two different [ear, nose, and throat] doctors who told us she needed tubes. I just did not feel right doing that to my baby, so we tried the alternative route and it worked!

Since, like Lisa, I already had one child who had cruised through babyhood almost infection-free, I knew Ezra's troubles were probably not due to any oversight on my part. But as a mom, I still felt guilty. What was I doing wrong? Not too much, other than occasionally letting him lie down and drink a bottle, which can apparently lead to fluid buildup in his ear canal. Another factor that may have lead to Ezra's infections was that Jonah was in preschool two days a week, and both of them went to a baby-sitter a couple of times a week while I worked. Jonah was catching more bugs and passing them on to Ez. But the biggest reason for the disparity in my boys' health was probably the shape of their ears. According to our wise and wonderful pediatrician, Dr. Addy, some babies just have more steeply slanted ear canals, which makes them prone to fluid buildup, which makes every cold a potential ear infection.

My friend Ann went through the gamut with her older son, Jay, and now her baby, Jared. "It seemed as if I was taking Jay to the doctor every

 **A Word About Earwax**

Yup, it's gross, especially now that you have to deal with not only your own, but also with the waxy buildup of another human being. A normal amount is a good thing because it traps dirt, dust, and other potentially harmful particles before they get to the eardrum. But too much wax can be a problem, leading to muffled hearing. Remember what Mom said about not sticking anything in your ear smaller than your elbow? That little maxim has stood the test of time. It's tempting to poke a Q-Tip around in there, but don't: You may actually rupture Baby's eardrum. Instead, tilt Baby's head and drip hydrogen peroxide, or mineral or baby oil, in his ear. You might want to try this when he's asleep. Another way to deal with this is to get your doctor to flush Baby's ear with warm liquid or scrape out the wax. (Don't worry, she's trained to do this!)

six weeks when he was a baby," she remembers. "Finally the doctor prescribed this wonderful decongestant, Rinatin, which cleared the fluid in
Jay's ears. Now, with Jared, I ask for it almost right away. I also give him
Augmentin, which he hates and which gives him diarrhea. I just kind of
bite the bullet, tip him backwards, restrain his arms, and squirt the medicine in his mouth. Of course he's crying at this point, but it goes down.
For the diarrhea side effect, feeding him banana slices with the medicine
kind of counteracts the problem."

If your beloved baby has the symptoms of an ear infection—pulling on
her ear, crying, fever, waking up at night—take her to the doctor right
away. It's important to stay on top of repeated ear infections to prevent possible long-term damage to her hearing. You and your pediatrician can plot
which course of treatment to take—watchful waiting, pink stuff, white
stuff, decongestant, pain relievers, homeopathic treatments, and so on.

Acetaminophen (such as infant Tylenol), ear-numbing drops (available by prescription only), or warm oil drops can make a dent in your
baby's pain. Some parents absolutely love those numbing drops, although
you'll have to check with your own doc and see what he/she says about
them. You might also try placing a warm (not hot) washcloth against
Baby's ear as a comfort measure.

Sweet Willow Grace,

From the first time I knew that you grew inside me, you have brought such joy to my heart. I don't want to believe that you are already seven months old. Right now you're swinging gently in your swing, kicking your feet and clapping your hands with joyous abandon that I envy so. My heart is melted by your four-toothed grin, by your first attempts to crawl as you lift up on all fours only to fall forward with each push of your legs. When your sisters get off the big yellow school bus, you laugh, and your whole body shakes with excitement. You sit and play, content to bang your toys or suck on anything within reach. And when you grow tired, you rub your eyes with both fists and shake your head back and forth, back and forth until you doze off.

When I found out we were going to have you, it came as a surprise. I'd thought we were all done having babies. And yet I see God's wisdom in sending you to us. I didn't know how much we needed you. You have reminded me of the important things in life—to trust my heavenly Father to care for me just as you trust me to care for you. You keep me focused on the meaning of life and the One who loves me so deeply. The One who sent you. He knew we would need your smiles and coos in this past year when we lost Grandma. God shows us His love every day—I see Jesus in you.

As you grow, never lose sight of the important things in your life—the people who love you, the Lord who died to save you. Because just as you are a gift to me, you are a gift to the world—your smile for starters and, beyond that, a universe of potential all bottled into your twenty-pounds-clothed-in-pink-footie-pajamas.

My promise to you, my sweet Willow Grace, is that I will always, always love you, always believe in you, always pray for you.

Love,

Mom

—Traci DePree, mother of Caitlin,

Megan, Haley, and Willow

# Fat? PHAT! and Fun, Fun, Fun

*Milemarker!* "You've always known that you and your baby are two separate creatures, but she hasn't. To her, the two of you are one—she has no identity of her own. When you put her in front of a mirror, she doesn't even realize that the baby she sees is her. But this month she'll make a huge mental leap and finally understand that she's an individual, with her own body, thoughts, and feelings. This jump in understanding opens the door to her growing emotional and physical independence, which will take years to fully develop."[1]

## Getting Your Body Back

It was one of those "aye yi *yi*" moments indelibly engraved on my consciousness. I joined a gym and, as part of the membership deal, was able to spend an hour with a personal-trainer type to "assess" my bod, evaluating exactly what needed to happen for said bod to get buff. Of course, I had the wrong shoes, right off the bat. Having never been much of a workout fiend, I didn't own any shoes that were remotely right for exercising. So there I was, wearing baggy sweats and these vaguely sneakery-looking things (I think they were suede) and bracing myself for the perky chick with the ripped abs to put me through my paces.

"Hi, I'm Mike. I'm going to be doing your fitness evaluation today."

Gulp. He had ripped abs all right, but he wasn't female. In fact, before me stood one of God's gifts to womankind, a guy so dazzling I could barely speak. (You know by now I'm happily married, and I love Doyle dearly. What I'm telling you ladies is, this guy was amazing, and anyone, even a contented matron such as myself, would have been unhinged by this person's attractiveness. You know Tom Cruise? Getting warmer.)

"Oh," I managed, peeking again at my ridiculous footwear and decidedly unhip clothing. It was going to take all my poise—and I've never had much—to get through the next hour with Mr. Perfection.

"Get a grip, girl! This is a fitness professional, after all. He's probably seen flabbier than you in his day" was my pep talk to myself. Of course, as I cast a furtive glance around, there seemed to be only Victoria's Secret models and twenty-one-year-old tennis scholarship recipients prancing around. So much for that.

Mike was, in addition to his physical attributes, a warm and friendly guy. Of course he wasn't a slime ball, which would have made everything so much easier! He was patient with my fumbling attempts to maneuver the weight and cardio machines. "What are the problem areas you'd like to work on here at the gym?" he asked, sincerity oozing out of his every perfect pore.

"Oh, um, well…"

Problem areas! Like I am going to discuss the size of my posterior with this man! Not a chance.

"I guess just overall toning," I said, hoping he would leave it at that.

"Of course, of course. But I mean, specific areas of your body that concern you."

My entire body concerned me, actually.

My mind raced, trying to conjure up a limb or section on my physique I actually felt comfortable discussing. My worst fear was that I would blurt out the true, serious area of concern and have him measure it or pinch it with one of those barbarian fat tongs, only to gently break the news to me that said area was beyond any chart or evaluative graph to his knowledge. Oh, to have had the perky size-four trainer named Ashley instead!

My arms and knees are actually pretty decent, as limbs go, semi-toned and presentable, but I just couldn't bring myself to lie and tell him those were my problem areas. He just looked so, so genuine, so deeply concerned about my fitness welfare, I couldn't lowball good ol' Mike.

"My thighs, I guess, maybe," I stammered, much like Hugh Grant in any scene where he is professing his true feelings for his leading lady.

"Your thighs? Okay, let's work on your thighs."

You agreed to that a little too quickly there, Bubba.

My cheeks now a shade somewhere between mango pink and eggplant purple, I underwent a series of mortifying toning exercises, under Mike's dutiful tutelage.

Then this amazon man/instructor of the ever-hideous "fire hydrant" exercise kindly inquired if I was also interested in weight loss as part of my goals as a new gym member.

Well, yeah. Duh!

"It's been harder than usual to lose weight," I confided. "Ever since the birth of my son."

 **That's Saying It, Baby!**

Why can babies do some of the motions to ditties such as "The Itsy-Bitsy Spider" and "Pat-a-Cake" when they can't even say so much as "pat" yet? According to a new and trendy movement started by Dr. Joseph Garcia, because the words are accompanied by hand and body motions, preverbal babies can remember them better and participate in the songs. Classes in "baby sign language" are sprouting up like crabgrass all over the place as Garcia-trained teachers show moms and dads how to get their babies—as young as seven or eight months—to express their needs and observations through sign language before they can speak. Check out Dr. Garcia's Web site at www.sign2me.com.

"Of course," Mike crooned sympathetically. "After all, you just had a baby."

Yeah, twenty-six months ago! He must have thought I said my baby was two months old, not two years old.

"Right! Absolutely! Yes! You are right!" I said enthusiastically. After all, why in the world would I disabuse this nice fellow of his mistaken notion? This way, I could leave, a little sweatier, more rosy-cheeked, and still wearing ludicrous shoes, yet with a fiber of dignity still intact. I had had a baby recently! Which explained—yeah, rationalized—my additional *avoirdupois*. What a break!

"It was nice to meet you," Mike said in closing, shaking my hand. "You, too," I said. And I meant it because not only was he divinely handsome, but he felt, obviously, that I had an excuse for being a tad unbuff. What a guy, that Mike!

"Oh, and one more thing," he said just as I was about to bolt out the door to the safety of my car, littered with the flotsam and jetsam of my fast-food lunch. "You might want to invest in some good workout shoes. I wouldn't want you to get injured."

## Ditch the Stress of Dieting

That little episode went down about two years ago. I did in fact purchase some good workout shoes, not to mention logged many hours at the gym, burning my thighs on the ol' "fire hydrant." And boy oh boy! You should see my thighs now! They look about 9 percent better than they did that memorable day with Mike, but then again I've since delivered another child. (Excuses, excuses!)

For most of us, losing weight after the baby is of vital concern. Even for women who work valiantly at being "in the world and not of it," who love their Father in heaven dearly and live to serve Him, body image is a big deal.

**Voices**

"I gained a whopping sixty pounds (could be more, but I conveniently lost track in the eighth month) with our first child. I carried a good amount of extra weight until my second pregnancy, when I gained another sixty pounds—on top of the weight I never lost! Feeling desperate and without adequate clothes to return to work, I began to exercise regularly and diet. A year after Baby Number Two, I was below my original weight and felt great. Then an unexpected third pregnancy came along. This time, however, I gained less weight and lost most of it within six months after delivery. Losing baby weight was extremely difficult for me. I still do not understand how I gained so much (honest!) so quickly. I think it is difficult to get psychologically motivated to seriously lose weight when you're planning more pregnancies. When I thought I was done with childbearing, I had a serious desire to 'get back to normal,' and this ended up paying off."

—Lisa, 34

"All I can say is that it's in the genes! I'm the one-in-a-million pregnant woman who has to work at gaining weight during her pregnancy. I switch from skim to whole milk just so I get that extra fat intake. So far I have left the hospital in my prepregnancy jeans, and I consciously need to increase my food supply while I am nursing in order to maintain my weight. Some people are blessed with lots of money, some with big brains. I guess I've been blessed to be a middle-class, happy-to-finish-a-crossword-puzzle mom with a great metabolism and a knack for finding a good deal! I wouldn't ask for anything more!"

—Margaret, 29

Even with our eyes fixed on treasures of heaven, we're still earthbound creatures. It's just plain hard to dismiss the experience of not being able to squeeze into one's old pants. My friend's hardy-har-har brother-in-law used to joke that his wife could fit into her jeans, but not without a jar of Vaseline, a tow truck, and a German shepherd. (No word on whether, after years of those remarks, he's still allowed to sleep in the house!) In the months after I had my boys, I sometimes felt as if even a ton of motorized steel and all the lubricants in the world wouldn't help me jam my outsized bod into my pre-baby clothes.

With Jonah, I gained a modest twenty-six pounds, yet it took me about eighteen months to fully shed the surplus. Friends who had added forty, fifty, and more pounds slenderized faster than I. Of course, I did put on a few extra pounds months after the birth. During my pregnancy with Ezra, I packed on thirty-six pounds despite working out regularly throughout my term. And it's not exactly been smooth sailing trimming down this time either. I've tried various diets: eating cereal for two meals a day, drinking those meal substitution shakes, and cutting way down on breads, pastas, potatoes, rice (my favorite foods on the planet). All of these efforts have basically amounted to the proverbial hill of beans.

That's why I was so abundantly relieved and thoroughly delighted to discover the wisdom of Debra Waterhouse, author of *Outsmarting the Female Fat Cell—After Pregnancy.* Her "Postpartum Peace Plan" is the sanest, most realistic, and most reassuring new-mom weight-loss plan I've seen (more on this in a moment). Her research reveals that, as postpartum women, we are perhaps even more vulnerable to food issues than our fifteen-year-old baby-sitters:

> The University of Oxford in England found that pregnancy was
> one of the strongest life events to trigger an eating disorder. You
> may not have an eating disorder, but you may be a disordered eater,
> meaning you have an unhealthy relationship with food and your
> body. Most women are disordered eaters. 90 percent of us diet,

96 percent dislike our bodies, 80 percent fear weight gain, and 60 percent feel guilty when we've eaten our favorite foods.

We've matured into adults thinking that dieting, body dissatisfaction, and food fears are a normal part of being a woman. Well, there's nothing normal about waking up every morning hating your body, eating salad with fat-free dressing for lunch, or avoiding any event that calls for a bathing suit.[2]

I strongly recommend Waterhouse's book if you're in the 90 percent of women who struggle with body acceptance. Hearing the news that my fat cells had enlarged considerably since giving birth and would fight to the death before giving themselves up gave me a good, old-fashioned reassuring dose of reality. Finally, I knew what my body was "thinking," plus I had real ways to outsmart it. Get the book! You won't be sorry.

In the meantime, I've culled some highlights from her "Peace Plan," which has nada to do with weighing meat, banning whole food groups, or thinking sugar is evil. She has so completely influenced my own views on weight loss that it's impossible for me to give you my tips without giving her much of the credit.

First, *think small, not exclusive.* I know, I know. You've got everyone from Jennifer Aniston to your mother-in-law raving about The Zone diet or some other low-carb program. But as Waterhouse points out, it's not about axing carbs or fats or sugars; weight loss is really about portion savvy. Eat what you like, but in smallish-to-regular portions. "If your meals are small, you'll become a smaller postpartum woman," Waterhouse says.[3]

Here's the bonus: To rev up your sagging metabolism, now a sluggardly 15 to 25 percent slower than in your pre-baby days, throw fuel on the fire by eating four to six smaller meals a day. This is especially important if you're over thirty. Unfair but true: Your twenty-three-year-old sister-in-law can wolf down a side of beef and brownies for dessert and burn it off with little trouble. (Remember, you love her! She was your junior bridesmaid ten years ago!) You, on the other hand, my thirty-some-thing friend, burn off less than half of what she can with the same effort. So instead of taxing your body by scarfing down a Whopper and fries, eat a Whopper Jr. instead and skip the fries. You'll still be satisfied, and your body can much more effectively burn it off. Eating more often and still losing weight? Life is good!

Second, *relax.* "When we are stressed out, we stress out our fat cells," writes Waterhouse, "and they respond by shutting down fat release and turning on the storage again."[4] It's a scientific fact: People who manage their stress lose more weight. Calm yourself by taking deep breaths when you feel uptight, avail yourself of friends and family members who want to help (see "On the Relationship Seat" on page 124), and get out of the house regularly. Stress, I now believe, was the reason I packed on extra pounds after I had Jonah. Overwhelmed by a colicky infant and cooped up alone in the winter while Doyle worked second shift, I was stressed out, bored, and anxious, which led me to some serious stress eating. Check out "Sabotage Stress" in Month 12 (see page 203) for more tips on stress relief.

And third: *Move it, girl!* I don't know about you, but I'd rather work out a lot than subsisting on a liquid diet or cereal or cabbage soup. I've become proexercise and antidieting due to Waterhouse's winning strate-gies. "If you gained a lot of weight...please don't waste any more time beating yourself up," she writes. "Instead, beat the pavement and get out there and walk, stroll your baby, or run if that's your thing—just move!"[5] Working out with weights is something you can do at home, and there's nothing like it for accelerating your metabolism even while you sleep! Take it slow at first and work your way up to forty-five minutes of aerobic exer-cise every other day. According to Waterhouse, your postpartum fat cells don't even wake up until you've been exercising for thirty minutes. Each minute over thirty, she says, is a fat-burning one. "Can't make it straight through the whole sixty-minute workout video?" she writes. "Go straight to the ab portion one day and the cardio the next. At least you'll feel like you're doing something."[6]

Walking worked for my friend Laura, who gained fifty-five pounds during her pregnancy. "It took me a year to get back to my pre-baby weight. Then I lost another few pounds after that," says Laura. "I walked every day, weather permitting, after Amelia was born. I think we started walking when she was about two weeks old, after I was nearly all healed up." Exercise also releases those warm-fuzzy hormones, endorphins, soothing your stresses, helping you snooze at night, and giving you the option of treating yourself with something gooey and decadent once in a while. After all, you've worked for it.

Another idea is to get a recommended postpartum workout video or a Pilates or yoga program (of the nonspiritual variety) to do while Baby naps.

If you're breast-feeding, don't quit now. New studies show it's the length of time you breast-feed that contributes to weight loss. Those who nurse from six to twelve months lost more weight than new moms who threw in the towel at six months. Actually, bottle-feeders weigh less than women who breast-feed for six months or less. Take it from my wonderful

 **Tooth Care for Little Tykes**

I have a pal who used to brush her cat's teeth with this liver-smelling paste concocted just for felines. Apparently cats are not fans of mint like the rest of us. To be frank, I have never brushed Pierre's teeth. For one thing, I value the use of my hands too much. Once my friend had her first baby, though, you know what happened: The kitty's bicuspids could have rotted in his head for all she cared. She does brush her baby's teeth, though, and so should you. Skip the fluoridated paste and brush Baby's teeth and gums with water or special baby/toddler toothpaste. Wiping them with a soft washcloth or gauze also works. When he's three or four, take him to the dentist (the kid, not the cat).

cousin-in-law, Alanna: "I nursed Bennett until thirteen months, and he sucked everything out of me. I'm twenty pounds less now than my pre-pregnancy weight. Now that I'm finished, I have to be careful how I eat, as far as amounts and sweets goes. So really, that was a fairly effortless weight loss plan for me."

Now more than ever learn to embrace your new body: "It's so easy to embrace your body for its miraculous life-giving ability right after birth," Waterhouse writes. "But as the weeks and months pass, you're bound to be frustrated with it for not losing weight and regaining shape."[7] Listen, we have given birth to these beautiful, precious babies, and we should be proud of our bodies, seriously. Think PHAT (my version is "Pretty Hip and Terrific"), not fat! True, my twice-C-sectioned tummy will never look like Britney Spears' abs—not that they ever did—but my two gorgeous little guys are well worth it. All we can do is try to eat healthfully, exercise for all the right reasons, and regard our changing physiques with acceptance and even pride. By not dieting and embracing your new postpartum body, you'll be sending the valuable—and sadly, rare—message to your little ones, girls or boys, that you're happy with the body God gave you. This message is a true gift and a way of honoring your body's Maker.

## On the Relationship Seat: It Takes Two to Train

Every journey is better shared, and that goes double for your trip back to your pre-baby body—or even to a healthier, stronger body. Ask a girl-friend to walk with you a few days a week or vow to bug each other to hit the gym. Personal trainers, once the sole province of people like Cher and Madonna, are now available to slobs like you and me for thirty to fifty dollars per hour through your local gym. You may balk at the price, but a good trainer can customize a workout for you in one hour that you can do alone from then on.

Your best workout buddy is your baby, who can enjoy a brisk stroller cruise while you burn calories and build muscle. "Mommy and Me" exercise classes designed for moms with infants are often offered by local recreation centers, YMCAs, and even churches. Can't find a class? Buy a mom-plus-baby video, such as *The Complete Body Workout for Mom and Baby* (available at www.amazon.com), and invite a fellow mommy or two over for a workout in your living room.

My friend Patti employed her kids as walking workout buddies. "With Becca, I was smaller within two weeks after I delivered than when I got pregnant. I wore home my regular jeans from the hospital after having Drew, but the third baby, Breanna, was a different story! It took me fourteen to fifteen months to lose the weight after that one, and all I did was walk for at least thirty minutes about six days a week, pushing my two babies (one and two years old) in a double stroller. Weight training to boot!"

## Just a Few of Many Ways to Make a Baby Laugh

"Bring a baby to a grownup—even the gruffest and most inhibited—and watch what happens. Without exception, they will do something to try and make the baby laugh. Psychologists, anthropologists and other experts have theories about why this is so. For me it's enough to believe that whenever baby laughs, our humanity is somehow exalted."[8]

Jack Moore is a funny, funny guy. I mention this because he's written a marvelous little tome called *97 Ways to Make a Baby Laugh,* and it just oozes charm and elicits giggles. You know this already: Your baby's laugh is the most glorious sound in the world. Any baby's chuckle is delightful, but when it's your own cutie pie—well, don't get me started.

Certainly, it would be nice to now quote Jack Moore's book in totality because there's no way on God's green earth I could come up with ideas anywhere near as cute and adorable as his. But, well, it's kind of illegal to do that, and besides, I want you dash off to your friendly neighborhood bookstore and buy his book!

However, since I cannot handle suspense of any kind, I have included below three of his winsome suggestions for evoking that sound of sounds, your darling's incomparable chortle:

*#2. The Disappearing Noodle:* Place the end of a long strand of spaghetti in Dad's mouth and have him suck it in as quickly as possible. (Note: for best results, I prefer cappellini done al dente, but I have friends who swear by linguine.)

*#8. Put on a polka cassette or CD and do the polka with your spouse.* (But only if you have absolutely no idea how to actually do the polka.) There is something inherently funny about bad polka dancers. Just do it.

 **Brain-Boosting Toys for Six- to Nine-Month-Olds**

- *Busy board.* Many babies delight in these activity boards that can be attached to a crib rail. In addition to helping him practice hand-eye coordination, the busy-board toy may trigger a big light-bulb moment: Baby can make things happen—sounds, lights, movement!—when he prods, twists, squeezes, shakes, or flips the thing.
- *Soft dolls or stuffed animals.* Baby's ripe for picking a "lovey," a favorite stuffed animal or blanket. You'll be amazed at "who" she selects because it won't be that adorable, forty-dollar, brand-name, unbelievably soft giraffe your infantless sister-in-law bought her. Jonah chose as his lovey a nondescript teddy bear who used to warble "Jesus Loves Me," but after a few washes is mute and raggedy. Whoever Baby's chosen one is, make sure it's free of potential choking hazards like loose eyeballs, buttons, and ribbons.

*#92. Using Your Noggin.* Attach a suction cup toy—like the one on Baby's high chair tray—to your forehead. Baby will find this trick—and you—a laugh riot.[9]

If you are living on an Amish colony, substitute German egg noodles for cappellini. In lieu of dancing, which is likely not allowed, you may want to try extremely vigorous canning. Finally, as an alternate to toys with suction cups, try draping a long egg noodle over your forehead and see if Baby notices. Or maybe put a pickle in each ear and stick out your tongue. That oughta do it. (And if Elder Yoder drives by in his buggy, for heaven's sake, duck!)

My personal favorite is the Stinky Feet activity, where one pretends to smell Baby's footsies (which smell approximately like the rest of him), say "eeee-EWWWWW" with great dramatic force, and then fall over as if

- *Balls.* "Ball" was one of Ezra's first words, and though he didn't utter it until he was about a year old, he had already gotten plenty of enjoyment out of various balls rolling around the house. Roll one back and forth between the two of you on the floor, or when your baby is older, toss it across the room so he can crawl after it.
- *Household items.* There's a reason babies are famous for banging pots and pans: They love 'em! A few bowls, spoons, and kitchen doodads will amuse Baby for an astonishing amount of time and allow you to whip up your famous pear tart with crème fraîche (or microwave popcorn—whichever).
- *Wood or soft blocks.* Monkey see, monkey do. Demonstrate how to stack a few blocks and then knock them down. Heap them into containers for him and dump them out. He'll get the picture that this is a hugely fun thing to do.

asphyxiated. After about two dozen performances at my house, though, Ezra got kind of jaded. Now I get a smirk, maybe, for my efforts. But, hey, at least one of us is having fun!

I also do this thing where I swing my hair onto my face and put on sunglasses or something, like Cousin Itt from *The Addams Family*. Usually the incongruity of it all strikes my audience of one as highly humorous, if I do say so myself.

If you're worried that you really, truly are not a person imbued with a discernible sense of humor, that your personality is about as captivating as teething toast, don't despair. You, too, can perform hilarious sight gags and make your offspring convulse in laughter! The key is loosening up and having a wonderful time with your baby. Chances are, he will think you're a laugh riot: "What a scream my mommy is! Ah, the merriment, the hilarity, the snickering that goes on at our house!" Plus, one benefit here is that if you go too far, get too jiggy with it, and Baby pees his pants, it's not a problem, what with his current lack of bladder control and all. If this happens to your husband, well, that's a bit more of a problem.

# The Top Ten Ways
# to Make the Kid Crack Up

### 1. Noodle Through the Nostrils
I had an ex-boyfriend who did this, and, well, we broke up. But his little parlor game had a certain element of gross humor.

### 2. Beverage Through the Nostrils
Again with the nostrils, make your beverage of choice spew out of them, causing you to sputter violently and Baby to giggle. (Fun with nostrils!)

### 3. Oink Oink Oink
Make oinking noises. This just slays 'em.

## 4. Saturday Night Fever

Instead of the polka, insert your dance of choice. The cha-cha, the mambo, the hustle all work well. (Don't try the macarena, though. Hey, how 1997 is that? Puh-lease!)

## 5. Ppppllllllbbbbbbllllllpppp!

The classic raspberry: Blow on your baby's tummy, somewhere near the belly button, making the silliest noises known to mankind. This has a double benefit in that it's also a method of tickling.

## 6. Yummy!

"Can I eat your toes with ketchup?" said in a sprightly manner, followed by one-by-one toe nibbling and eating noises is great fun for all.

## 7. Upside Down Fun

Stand on your head, literally. (To be used as a last-ditch effort and only in the company of another grownup who can catch you as you come hurtling down to the ground.)

## 8. Buzz Like a Bee

Roll your eyes and make a buzzing bee sound while rolling your head around in circles. (Depending on your level of sleep deprivation, you may be doing this anyway.)

## 9. Yoooodeeeeelllllaaaayyyyheeeehoooo!

Er, what I mean to say is, give yodeling a try.

## 10. Silly Words

Say the word *babaganoush* in several different accents. Try Pepe Le Pew, Donald Duck on helium, Yogi Bear. Baby might look at you and think, *Um, okay,* but you may get a kick out of it.

Dear Peaches (a.k.a. Ava America Williams),

What happy days you have brought to your daddy and me, Baby Girl! Before I found out I was going to be a mama, I never in a million years would have guessed how satisfying taking care of a baby can be. You wake me up every morning now with your sweet sing-song babbling: "Ma-ma...ma-ma...ma-ma!" Your little voice gets more insistent as time wears on and Mama still hasn't rolled herself out of bed yet, but when I finally get to your crib, your chubby cheeks just split into the cutest little grin. It's like you're saying, "Hey, Mama! What took you so long?"

Then we have our breakfast, and I'll tell you, Peach, that whole process is getting more interesting every day since Dr. Singh told me to start you on finger foods. The first time I put some rice cake pieces and banana slices on your tray, you tried to stuff everything in your mouth at one time! And then last week you were not in the mood for finger foods, apparently, and in about two seconds you threw every bit of food onto the floor. (Nala, our dog, falls more in love with you with every "freebie" you throw her way!) So far sweet potatoes are your favorite food, and I'm going to ask Mama Lu to fix you her famous sweet potato pie when you get old enough.

We play peekaboo for awhile, or read some stories, and then after our nap, Daddy comes home for lunch. You are Daddy's baby girl, no question in my mind. He comes home with a big smile on his face, dying to see his "Miss America." Even if you're fussing, Daddy will charm the fuss right out with his smiles and tickles and kootchie coo. It's so funny that he calls you Miss America because I really had to work on him so he'd agree to name you after my great-great-great grandma, who was a slave in Mississippi. She was a brave and devout woman of God, and I wanted you to have her name.

Ava America "Peach" Williams: Never forget that your mama loves you, and so does your daddy, Mama Lu, Granny Geri, Papa Ardie, and, most of all, Jesus. Let Him be your rock and your salvation, Baby Girl, and you will have a wonderful life.

—Kendra Williams, mother of Ava

# Money Pits, Parsimony, and Peace

*Milemarker!* God created us to have a full complement of emotions: joy, anger, sadness, contentment. By now your baby's emotions have learned to manifest themselves. She may perform tricks, such as throwing a kiss to familiar people, and may encore if her performance is the hit she hopes it is. Over the next few months, Baby may learn to evaluate and mimic moods and might show the first stirrings of empathy. For instance, if she sees someone crying, she may start crying too. On the bright side, laughter is still and always will be much more contagious than tears.

## The New Money Pit

When Ezra was born, our shrewd lactation consultant fixed Doyle with one of those laser gazes. "If Lorilee nurses, you will save $1,000 in the next year," she said in an elaborately casual fashion, although the comment was anything but "by the way." Interestingly, her remark was targeted to him, not me, the milk spigot in the family. I know what she was up to, that wily lacto-maniac. She knew an effective way to drum up spousal support for nursing was to make an appeal to the new dad's checkbook. In our case, the tip didn't really apply (I combo fed, thus only saving about $300), but she did underscore one of the best cash-saving tips out there for Baby's first year: breast-feed.

"I nursed my kids, which saved hundreds on each child (probably thousands, if I added it up)," said Patti, mother of three. Actually, the average amount people spend on formula is about $850 per year, so Patti was right. She saved a whopping $2,500 over the course of three babies. "I figure I've saved a thousand dollars in really expensive formula by nursing the boys for a year," says Ann Elizabeth, a seasoned mom of four who bottle-fed her older two children and breast-fed her two little boys. "The benefits, besides saving money, include no gross formula burps right in your face and not so many formula stains on their clothes."

Saving money is one of the biggie issues for new parents. Not only are many of you adjusting to drastic budget slashes anyway, the loss of one income being what it is, but these cherubic, heart-stealing new family members are bona fide money pits. It's up to you, as the matriarch or patriarch of the clan, to throw cash around for such expenditures as food, clothing, shelter—little things like that.

## The Top Ten Ways to Save a Buck

Being slightly dense at parsimony—I usually wouldn't know a deal if it whacked me in the kneecap—I've asked some of my Thrift Queen buddies to weigh in. But before I unleash them in all their zealously frugal glory, I will take the time now to let you in on my best money-saving move: HAVE TWO BABIES OF THE SAME SEX EXACTLY THREE YEARS APART. Two years apart also works; the key here is to hit the same season. Of course, if you live in Negril or Nunavit for that matter, seasonal dressing is not an issue.

What about eBay? This Web site has been, for the Craker boys, a very slick source of fabulous, high-quality, brand-name kids' clothing for consignment store prices. Sometimes you can really get lucky, like the time I hit the jackpot with a Roots (a premium Canadian brand) sweatshirt and a Gap Sunday-go-to-meeting dress shirt for Ez. Both had been worn only once or twice and together cost me less than ten bucks with shipping. Brand new, those sharp duds would have set me back about fifty bucks.

Also, I've taken to hitting the high-end children's clothing shops during their seasonal clearances. When Ez was a newborn, I was prowling around a sales rack at Talbots Kids when I spotted a Columbia ski jacket, size eighteen months, reduced so rashly I thought I was hallucinating. But yes, that too-good-to-be-true winter parka was in fact seventeen dollars, down from its original price of eighty-eight dollars. Ezra wore that jacket for six months during his second winter, and it looks like it could be passed down to six more children, should I have six more children (which I won't). Of course, I started to get paranoid that people thought I actually paid eighty-eight dollars for a baby's jacket, which got me started explaining myself to nursery workers, relatives, and strangers alike.

Of course I don't want you to get the impression that money grows on trees around here—it doesn't—but as I said, bargain hunting is not my forte, sad but true. Thankfully, I have savvy pals who are gracious enough

## And You Thought College Was the Big-Ticket Item

What you'll probably spend on Baby's first year:

| | |
|---|---|
| Baby Clothes: | $500 |
| Baby Food, Formula: | $900 |
| Bedding, Décor: | $300 |
| Crib, Mattress, Dresser, Rocker: | $1,500 |
| Disposable Diapers: | $600 |
| Maternity/Nursing Clothes: | $1,200 |
| Nursery Items, Highchair, Toys: | $400 |
| Stroller, Car Seat, Carrier: | $300 |
| Miscellaneous: | $500 |
| **TOTAL:** | **$6,200**[1] |

to let me in on their little economies which, added up, can amount to big savings:

## 1. Go Natural

"I used cloth diapers. At twenty dollars a week for disposables, at least, cloth diapers were the way to go for our limited budget." —Patti

## 2. Go Old Fashioned

Wipe and wash the old-fashioned way. "Instead of using wipes for every diaper change, I half-filled a small bowl with water and a small squirt of liquid baby soap. (I used warm water the first few months and then room temperature after Baby could handle it.) I kept a ready supply of cloth diapers, baby facecloths, and thin towels cut into regular facecloth-size pieces. At change time I would drop one or two cloths into the water, wipe up any really dirty stuff with some Kleenex and then give the bum a good cleaning with the cloths. I think it saved us a lot of money. Of course I used the wet wipes when we'd go out, as well as when others took care of him here at home." —Alanna

## 3. Room to Grow

"Don't buy too many clothes in the small (birth-to-three-month) sizes; they will be outgrown too fast. If you get a lot of gifts in the same size, exchange some for larger sizes so you have something for your child to move up into. Also, a friend lent us some cute clothes that her boys got to wear only a few times because they grew so fast." —Ann B.

## 4. Rummage a Bit

"Thrift stores, yard sales, thrift stores! By the item, by the bag, by the pound—you can't really get any better deals when it comes to kids' items, especially clothes. If you're looking for that specific item, in that particular color, with that unique label, you might still be looking. But if you can plan ahead and know your quality, then secondhand is the way to go.

"I have plastic garbage cans in my attic, bigger and cheaper than storage bins, labeled with the different sizes. When I find a 'keeper' at a sale, I wash it and toss it into the correct can for later use. You will have a wonderful surprise when your child reaches that size and your 'barrel' is waiting and ready to go. Don't ever buy anything that needs a button or some surgical procedure. You won't fix it and will spend more money trying to than you paid. But if someone gives you free stuff, never turn it down! Just go through it, use what you can, pass along what you can't, and toss what you don't like. The next free load might be full of treasures, and they won't think of you again if you were too good for the first load." —Margaret

## 5. Secondhand Brands
Buy brands secondhand. "I shopped a ton at Value Village [a Canadian consignment store chain] for baby clothes. When babies are small they wear clothes for such a short time that they don't get worn out. I found some fabulous designer clothes that were nearly brand new!" —Laura

## 6. Think Simple and Comfy
"Forget the fancy clothes and shoes. Invest in lots of cute sleepers and rompers in soft cotton fabric. Babies like them better anyway, and they don't cost nearly so much. As for shoes, most babies kick them off anyway after about three seconds. Just get little booties or have them crawl around in socks until they are walking outside." —Ann Elizabeth

## 7. Become a Borrower
"Borrow what you can. We borrowed a swing from a coworker instead of buying one. We get to use it as long as we need it, and we don't have to store it when Adam outgrows it." —Ann Baker. (My friend Ann Elizabeth echoes the wisdom: "Find someone who is willing to lend you their baby bathtub, jumpy seat, bath ring, whatever. You use them for such a short time that it's silly to spend the big bucks unless you're planning to have a bunch of kids, which I wasn't but did anyway!")

## 8. Clip Those Coupons: Phase One

"For disposable items like diapers and wipes, I am the coupon scout! I sign up for every free baby or parent magazine that I spot because, even though by now I can write half the articles, the coupons inside are phenomenal. I also ask friends and family who don't have babies to send me coupons. I use these along with the store coupons from the magazines for extra savings. You can always use a manufacturer coupon with a store coupon. You would be surprised at how much you can save on baby things if you just take that little extra time and map out your game plan." —Margaret

## 9. Clip Those Coupons: Phase Two

Sign up for those money-saving coupons from Similac and other formula manufacturers that you find in maternity-clothing stores and baby stores. Not only do you get coupons, but you get boxes of free formula. Even though I nursed, I kept formula on hand. I never bought a can for either boy because they came in the mail for free. I was giving them away."
—Ann Elizabeth

## 10. Huge Canisters of Formula

Okay, I'm back and actually bearing a money-saving tip: With Ez, I discovered the mondo-huge canisters of formula at places like Wal-Mart, Kmart, and Target. I figured I saved about five dollars every time I ventured to one of these stores for formula instead of grabbing a regular-sized can along with my groceries. It added up, plus we could feed our baby for about ten days without having to leave the house once for a formula run (great for blizzards!).

# $weet, $weet Nursery

Creating a nursery for my babies has been one of my all-time favorite parenting tasks. (If naming babies and decorating their rooms were all there

## A Little Common Cents

Leah Severson is the author of *Bargain Buys for Baby's First Year.* Now here is a woman blessed with common sense, the kind that women like me need to benefit from since we are sadly lacking it on our own. Here's what she had to tell us:

*Q: What's the biggest overhyped product out there today for babies, in your opinion?*
A: The Diaper Genie. I hardly ever change my baby's diaper in her room anyway. It's always on the living room floor someplace, so that's one thing. The replacement bags for the Genie will run you about three hundred in the two-and-a-half years you will be changing diapers. I just use empty bread bags or newspaper tube bags to tie up dirty diapers and then throw them in the garbage or a pail. It's much cheaper.

Second, convertible cribs are not a bargain at all. They give you just the bed frame, so you have to buy a mattress anyway, and if you have another baby, where is she supposed to sleep? Just buy a crib and then a twin bed when your baby is ready for it.

*Q: I fell for the Carnation Formula trick two babies in a row! How does that work?*
A: My sister-in-law fell for it three babies in a row! Those cans of formula are tricky. They look like they're the same size, but they make different quantities of formula. The Carnation Good Start formula has twelve ounces of powder in it, while other brands, like Similac and Isomil, have fourteen ounces and make more formula per can. [Although less expensive per can], when you break it down by the number of ounces it makes, Carnation is the most expensive per ounce. Also on the topic of formula, go for the store brands, not the name brands. Many of the store brands of formula, like Kmart's, are made by Wyeth Pharmaceuticals, the same

company that makes the top brands. It's all regulated, and it's not as if [the big discount chains] are shipping your formula out of some Third World country.

*Q: What is the biggest spending trap new parents fall into?*
A: The crib stuff [accessories like bumper pads, quilts, dust ruffles]. The National Institute of Health tells us not to buy quilts and comforters and bumper pads for our babies because they could suffocate. Several babies have died in the last few years by burying their faces into bumper pads. Plus, the strings pose a choking hazard. I mean, a three- or four-month-old baby is not going to ram her face or head into the crib slats so hard she causes injury! You just don't need them, as cute as they are.

*Q: What do you think of the new premium brand diapers that offer diaper-rash protection?*
A: A pediatrician told me that if your baby has a diaper rash, put Vaseline on it and change her often. The amount of petroleum or whatever in these diapers that actually rubs off onto Baby's skin is not enough to treat a real diaper rash.

*Q: What's your best money-saving tip that's also super convenient?*
A: Those little premeasured formula packets are expensive. Just premeasure them yourself and scoop the right amount into little plastic bags.

*Q: Those little rug rats need to be clothed. Any hot tips for baby fashionistas?*
A: With my second baby, I learned to buy better quality clothes. If you buy good quality the first time, you can wash and wash those clothes and pass them on to the next baby and even the next. I buy 90 percent of my girls' clothes at consignment shops. I have gotten great brand names—Polo, Hilfiger, Lands' End—and they last from one baby to the next. This is also cheaper than buying lower-grade quality clothes at Wal-Mart or Target and paying full price. In the summer, I would buy oversized

T-shirts, say a year ahead in terms of size, and fasten them between their legs to make a cheap yet adorable romper. Then the next summer the item would still have lots of use left as a T-shirt. Buy quality here!

*Q: As the queen of bargains, do you have any overpriced skeletons in your closet, so to speak?*

A: Well, just the other day, my husband came home with Pampers—in broad daylight! I said, "What if someone had seen you?" Also, I fell in love with a forty-five-dollar lamp for my second daughter's room. I think I felt guilty because her room is nothing like her older sister's nursery was. I'm not even taking any pictures of her room because I want to say someday, "Your room was so beautiful. Too bad we have no pictures." So I bought this lamp with glow-in-the-dark stars on it, and it went against everything I believe in. The worst part is, it doesn't even work. My older daughter knocked it over, and it's never worked since. A fifteen-dollar lamp from Wal-Mart? That would still work.

was to this parenting gig, I'd have seventeen kids.) I always tell people that decorating is my only domestic skill, and sadly, this is all too true. At any rate, being impractical, I didn't just throw Baby Boy #2 into the same room as Baby Boy #1. Nope. I needed to "do" a nursery for Ez, too. Never mind that we thought he was going to be a girl. When he arrived on this earth bearing the markings of the male species, I had a theme picked out and ready to go. Jonah's motif was polar bears, which has segued nicely into a Yukon-Wildlife-Hockey kind of scheme as he grew. Clearly, this arctic décor would clash badly with my new brainwave: Farm. I couldn't see blending the two into some sort of Tundra-Cow-Fusion thing. (You should also know that Doyle thinks I'm a bit nuts about this whole theme thing, but in the interest of marital goodwill, he rolls with it.) So Ez inhabits a tiny little room, formerly my office. I spruced it up with a nifty cow rug, a brightly colored quilt with chickens and barns and whatnot, and— the pièce de résistance—a framed, blown-up color photo of my Grandpa Loewen driving his bright red combine in a field of golden flax under a prairie blue sky. Wow!

I purchased the two big-ticket items, the rug and the quilt, for half price after watching and waiting on the Internet for them to go on sale. EBay is also a wonderful place to find cool stuff for Baby's room, and Target seems to be honing in on the Pottery Barn scene with their own, much cheaper line of kiddie chic. "Forgo cutesy (and expensive!) nursery decorating for solid basics, and/or get creative," advises my friend Ann B. "I framed greeting cards illustrated with some of our favorite children's book characters for Adam's room as an inexpensive wall decor option." All that to say, you can be a décor fiend like me and still create a great space for your baby that won't dent your checkbook.

I love Leah Severson's admission that she paid way too much for her second daughter's lamp. I won't even tell you how much I paid for Jonah's "transition from baby to big boy" lamp. Let's just say I still feel guilty about it. Anytime someone comes over and we give them the grand tour, The Lamp is one of the major stops along the way: "And to your left, direct your attention to a massive monetary indiscretion/monument to foolishness/ridiculously expensive lighting fixture." Sigh.

At least it hasn't broken like Leah's lamp. Yet.

## On the Relationship Seat: The Prince of Peace

Is there anything in this world fiercer than a mother's feeling of protectiveness for her baby? We look down in wonder at our bundles, wrapped snugly in blankets, as they exude helplessness with the very rising and falling of their tiny chests. And our hearts lurch at the thought of anything remotely negative touching this new life, entrusted to us for protection and care. Thank God there is Someone so much stronger and wiser than us mere mortals holding our babies in His arms. What a relief to know we can go to Him anytime—in the middle of a bleary-eyed night, while bathing our slippery-when-wet munchkins, or when driving to the doctor for the hideous first round of vaccines.

In her book *Praying the Bible for Your Baby*, Heather Harpham Kopp points out that even when we're incoherent with fatigue or hormone-induced paranoia, our Father knows the cries of our hearts. "He is the perfect conversationalist, even when we're not. Our heavenly Father hears the unspoken longings behind our halting words—especially the ones that simply cry, 'Abba! Father!'"[2]

When I was a brand-new, wet-behind-the-ears mom, I remember having these miniseizures of paranoia about something bad happening to my Jonah. At the time we lived in a beautiful old home in a fringe neighborhood of the city. Most of the time I felt perfectly safe there, having picked up some street smarts during my college years in Chicago. But that was before I had Jonah. Now a drug bust five blocks away was way too close for comfort. And the suspiciously strung-out-looking woman who had moved in across the street, into the block's one "bad apple" house? I wished she would disappear, far away from my baby. So much for having a heart for ministry! Irrational thoughts would flitz through my postpartum, hormone-addled brain, thoughts like "What if one of these druggies kidnaps my perfect baby for the black market?" I mean, truly wacky thoughts! Other moms have confessed their fears of cancer, autism, pedophiles, drunk drivers…things that could potentially harm their babies.

Bonnie, an old friend of mine from junior high, is now the seasoned mom of three. But she once was a scared newbie like the rest of us. Bonnie is one of those calm, quiet, steady-as-she-goes types who isn't given to bursts of imaginary tragedies. So I was surprised to learn that even she was susceptible to the New Mommy Fear Factor: When her firstborn, Suzanne, was tiny, Bonnie noticed a tiny scratch on her baby's little hand. Was she imagining things, or did the scratch get bigger with each passing day? Was it infected? Did Suzanne have…FLESH-EATING BACTERIA???!!!

Bonnie admitted that the thought did cross her mind. After all, Canadian political leader Lucien Bouchard actually had flesh-eating bacteria, somehow, and had lost a leg because of it. Suzanne is now nine years old, and Bonnie is happy to report her growing baby still has all her digits!

## Ain't Nobody Here But Us Chickens

I just couldn't help myself! Here's a bonus Top Ten for those of you who love the lists: "Things We Could Worry About but Probably Shouldn't."

### 1. Laundry Chute Accidents
You could forget what you're holding in each arm and accidentally throw the baby instead of his clothes down the laundry chute!

### 2. Tainted Breast Milk
In an effort to keep your innocent child far, far from the dangers of alcohol, you must politely inform your German neighbor Krimhilda that for Christmas this year, her famous peppermint schnapps fruitcake cannot be

partaken of for fear of the not insubstantial liquor getting into your breast milk and inebriating your baby. But then you might get headcheese as a gift instead!

### 3. Food-Borne Illness
You may have to eat the headcheese out of sheer politeness—and, it must be said, fear of Krimhilda herself—and you might develop a nasty strain of food-borne illness.

### 4. Flesh-Eating Bacteria
The scratch on Baby's cheek is not the result of unclipped fingernails but of…flesh-eating bacteria!

### 5. Diaper Detonations
The baby will, during his or her baptism or dedication, have a loud, colorful, unmistakable diaper detonation all over dear old Pastor Peavey.

### 6. Traveling Baby Poop
Pastor Peavey, a wonderful man of the cloth, though not a spring chicken, would *not notice* the fecal matter on his ichthus fish necktie and go on to hug numerous members of the congregation.

(Parenthetical anecdote: Our own pastor, Dave Beelen, tells a funny story of how he baptized an infant in our church and made a slight slip of the tongue he will never live down. At Madison Square Church, we have a tradition of having newly baptized babies carried off by two saintly pillars-of-the-church types to be viewed up close and personal by the flock who just promised to participate in the baby's spiritual growth. Folks close enough to the aisle can reach out a hand and pat the wee one's foot. Pastor Dave, having just doused a little churchgoing cherub, exhorted his congregation to "bless the baby on his bootie." It was only after about six hundred people starting giggling that the pastor realized just what he had said!)

## 7. Hurricanes!

In Kansas? C'mon!

## 8. Tornadoes!

In South Carolina? I don't think so.

## 9. Rare Nasal Disorders

Baby's sneezing fits, as cute as they are, are not really about getting out all that excess fluid in his body. Actually, they signal the onset of the rare nasal disorder your husband heard about once on the Discovery Channel.

## 10. Meat Thermometer Misuse

In your sleep-deprived state, you would accidentally use a meat thermometer to take your baby's temp, and he would forevermore feel slightly poultrylike in his deepest subconscious!

# You Hold the Baby; Let Jesus Hold You

Peace, part of the fruit of the Spirit, is described in John 14. This means that calmness, a state of mind not riddled with worries for your baby but rather filled with trust and hope, is a dividend of staying close to the Father.

"Peace I leave with you; my peace I give you. I do not give to you as the world gives. Do not let your hearts be troubled and do not be afraid" (John 14:27). These are words of life for everyone who believes, new parents included. Surrender your anxious thoughts about your baby's well-being to the One who made her and loves and adores her even more than you do. As one who struggles to find peace, a worrywart who so often slips away from the True Vine, I find real serenity sometimes fleeting. I cherish a line in one of the late Rich Mullins's songs: "Hold me, Jesus. I'm shaking like a leaf / You have been my King of Glory, won't you be my Prince of Peace?"

## Quotable

"Pour out your heart like water
in the presence of the Lord.
Lift up your hands to him
for the lives of your children."

—Lamentations 2:19

We trust Jesus for salvation, for reserving a spot for us in Gloryland, yet we struggle to rely on Him to care for our babies. True, in a flawed world steeped in original sin, terrible things happen, even to babies. It's hard to watch the news or crack open *Newsweek* or *Time,* what with the sad, sad things that hurt and destroy good people. But we have to remember, always and at every moment, that God is in charge and that nothing will befall our precious little ones without His say-so or His good intention. Surrender your fears about your baby to God. Just as your sweet child snuggles close to your heart, nestle into your Father's arms. Let His peace—that miraculous, confounding gift—infuse your life with its sweetness and strength. Pray "without ceasing" for your family and lean more and more on God's flawless wisdom and unfailing support.

Dear Mateo,

We just came back from your little cousin Pilar's baptism, and all the relatives kept saying how big you are. Compared to Pilar, who sleeps all the time and weighs about ten pounds, you are a chunk. And you are much more active than your baby cousin! Ever since you were six months old, when you started crawling, you have kept me on my toes. When we get together with my friends' babies, you seem to run in circles around them. When Hannah couldn't find her toy the other day, she just kind of looked for it and went back to sitting there, peacefully playing. Not you! If you lost one your toys, you would crawl as fast as you could until you found it. You might walk along the sofa or—you did this once already and gave me a heart attack—you could even stand alone for a minute, surveying your kingdom of toys.

On the plane last month to Puerto Rico, you were so squirmy I could barely hold on to you! Next time we go your papa is coming with us! But it was all worth it when we got to my grandmother's house, and all the relatives oohed and ahhed over you. My cousin Esteban couldn't believe how much you ate! No matter what he put in front of you, you gobbled it up like a starving bird. I can see already that you will eat us out of house and home someday. Maybe I should learn to cook, eh?

Your papa and I are constantly amazed at your go, go, go attitude. Mateo, you will never let anything or anyone stand in your way. It will be a great challenge for Papa and me to shape that strong will of yours and to teach you that sensitivity is the best way to balance strength.

You must know how very dearly we love you. It took so long for you to come to us, I was afraid we would spoil you rotten when you did come. Thank goodness you have such a strong personality, as it helps us remember that we can't give in to your every whim, or you'd become a little monster!

I am holding on to every moment with you, my precious son.

Love always,

Mama

—Karen Jimenez, mother of Mateo

# T. Berry, Travel,
# and Tipping Tiffany

*Milemarker!* "One or the other of the parents will arrive [at the nine-month appointment] ready to burst. 'Well, how are you?' I ask, waiting for the opening blast. 'Awful,' says the mother. 'Oh?' 'Yes, Alexander has totally fallen apart. He's either charging around, bawling, or sucking his thumb and glaring at me. He refuses the food I try to feed him. He just won't eat for me, and if you want the whole works, I'm not getting any sleep. He drives all day and all night. He wakes up at least once or twice every night. He's a mess and so am I!'"[1]

## "Touchpoint" Time

T. Berry Brazelton is one of my favorite go-to guys for parenting help. He's warm, reassuring, and wise, not to mention the fact that he's only a flip of the page away. If you haven't bought his classic *Touchpoints* yet, drop what you're doing and buy a copy. As a seasoned pediatrician, he knows babies inside and out. But Dr. T. Berry really shines because he understands the whole emotional realm of parenting. He will tell you not only why Baby's inner ear is prone to infections, but how this will affect his sleep, behavior, and development—and, even better, how your sleep, behavior, and development will be affected too!

You may not agree with him on every issue, but his wisdom will add layers of understanding to the complexities of bringing up your own one-of-a-kind baby.

Nine-month-olds, he says, are at a key "touchpoint," which means, basically, they are about to change like crazy, so you'd better be prepared. I love what Dr. T. Berry says about the nine-month doctor appointment, specifically the way Ms. Cool, Calm, and Collected (a.k.a. you and me) has become unglued by Baby's new groove.

A mess? Yup, that just about describes Ez and me when we hit this bump in the road. After the little stinker had yanked his spoon away from me for the fourteenth time, squawked blue murder at naptime for a week straight, and flung his bottle across the room, whacking the dog on the head, the truth suddenly dawned on me: "Gee, my child isn't as mild-mannered as I thought—and hoped." This realization was hard to take because with Ezra I had harbored a secret wish for one of those "easy" tots you hear about on television, at family gatherings, and in play groups. Sigh. I had to face the fact that, really, there wasn't a compliant bone in my secondborn son's body.

Thank goodness for Dr. T. Berry and his calm assurance that Ez was being vexatious and out of kilter because he was honing new competency levels in all kinds of skills and making a big leap to independence.

Still, Ez didn't want to be too autonomous, not yet. In the classic mode of a nine-month-old, Ez wanted me in clear view at all times. Your baby is probably the same. At this stage, she will likely shadow you around the house, content to play by herself only if you're in the same room. She needs regular assurance that all is peachy in her universe, which is still wrapped up tightly with yours.

One revelation of Baby's newfound self-sovereignty this month is that she may show signs of wanting to ditch the bottle or the breast. Unless you're totally ready to give up nursing or bottle-feeding, keep trying to get her interested again. She may very well decide in month ten that there's nothing better in the universe than breast milk or formula—what was she thinking? At this point, you'll kick yourself for drying up or giving all your bottles away to your pregnant sister. Plus, let's face it, there's not much sweeter in this world than cuddling your beloved babe during a feeding. Soon enough she'll be a toddler, racing through the house and eating pizza with the rest of the family.

She still needs the intimacy that feeding provides, and so do you. You may be dying to resume your normal, pre-breast-feeding life, where you didn't have to arrange your entire schedule around feedings. But if you're like most moms, you'll feel a pang of sadness when you think about those good old days of nursing. Plus, why rush your baby into growing up too soon? I've met more mothers who are absolutely, ferociously committed to switching their baby straight from breast to sippy cup, as if this will somehow ensure a lifetime of vibrant health, tremendous mental well-being, and probably a trip for four to Maui too.

You've got at least three months left of good bottle time, or breast-feeding, before it's even advisable to make the move to a cup. I'll tell ya, it's a heap of a lot harder to cradle a baby drinking out of a cup. The little rug rats just don't seem to want to tilt backward in the same, cozy, sweet, baby way.

Besides, your baby now has a grip on the idea that Daddy and teddy and the pet hamster all have a separate existence even when she cannot see them—that when someone leaves a room or the house, they are still around, just not with her. (Well, if the hamster leaves the house, there's not much hope he's coming back.)

Nine-monthers delight in playing simple games with family members or others. Don't worry if she can't quite figure out how to play with a certain toy—even an "age-appropriate" one. She will learn so much more about the way things work if you let her struggle with it herself, along with your gentle guidance and bolstering. If a big bro or sis lurks around, insisting Baby is doing it "wrong," try to get the message across that Baby has to learn on her own "just as you did when you were a baby." The main thing is, Baby is spending fun time with the ones she loves.

Right about now your baby's social skills are expanding, too. She can better gauge, for instance, if Mommy is in a good mood, Daddy's feeling playful, and Kitty's got that "Come near me and I'll scratch out your eyeballs" look. She's also more sensitive to sad emotions, and she may take up wailing in sympathy if another baby at daycare is falling apart.

I've heard certain moms brag that their baby began talking at this age. If one of your new-mother peers has issued such a statement on behalf of her prodigy, don't worry about your own munchkin's lack of loquaciousness. (This is the same parent who will, in the next couple of years, worry out loud that her brilliant two-year-old better slow down his learning curve or be way ahead of everyone else in kindergarten, bored because his classmates are so academically sluggish.)

About the most you can optimistically expect right now are a few pet syllables being tossed around the nursery, tried out for effect. For example, your baby might say "ba" for bottle, or "mamamamama," which may or may not mean you. Be thrilled with these first attempts at speech. He'll probably come out with a few real words in the next two or three months, but he may not actually begin to talk before the age of eighteen months or even two years.

What's more important is the fact that Baby understands what you say to her. (When Ms. Mommy-with-the-Mostest reveals how Junior blurted out the word "appendectomy" as she changed his diaper, you can throw in that your kid knows how to perform one.)

Experts say this is prime time to chat up Baby often, identifying familiar objects or giving her a play-by-play on what you're doing. Sooner than you can believe, she'll begin to comprehend words like *mommy, daddy,* and *bye-bye* and to follow simple instructions like "Wave bye-bye" or "Don't play in the garbage!"

Remember the pincer grasp, that huge milestone much touted in *What to Expect the First Year?* You know, the one where your baby could, sort of, pick up objects as small as a raisin with his thumb and forefinger? At this point, Baby is so over the pincer grasp. Now he's a professional pincer grasper. This is a good news/bad news kind of time. It means Curious

George can nab the tiniest objects around the house and examine them closely before popping them in his mouth. So you, as George's parent, have to be extravigilant about combing the floor for objects that can choke the little guy. But on the flip side, isn't it great that your baby is gaining so much dexterity? He can even fit his hand to the shape of the thing he's reaching for. You must call the grandparents and tell them about this pincer grasp thing. They'll be delighted.

## Planes, Trains, and Automobiles *(Avec Bébé)*

An acquaintance of mine likes to tell a tale of travel, a cautionary story that has stayed with me—lo, these four years of parenthood and henceforth into all seasons of lugging children about on trips. Apparently (and he wasn't really there, which may account for his zeal in recounting this little slice of life), this guy's wife was flying the friendly skies with two little ones under the age of two. Brave woman, and resourceful, as we shall see. She and her charges were seated in the aircraft's bulkhead, the best and roomiest locale for airborne babies and tots (more on that in a moment). Of course, moments after the flight attendants turned off the seatbelt sign and passengers were free to move about the cabin, one of the babes felt free to have a movement in his pants. (And this will happen to you, too, even if you changed a messy diaper seconds before boarding.) So Mom dutifully whipped out her changing pad and proceeded to change Junior's drawers.

 **I Can See Clearly Now**

Your baby's vision—previously about 20/40 at best—is now almost adultlike in its clarity and depth perception. Though his short-range sight is still better than his long-range acuity, his vision is good enough to recognize people and objects across a room.[2]

Wouldn't you know it, the little shyster produced the loose ball type of poop, not the compact and contained variety. Then, being a baby, he was not wont to emit only one BM at a time; instead, several perfect round little orbs popped out of him all at once, and not all of them landed in the diaper. You probably know where this story is headed—south, in the same direction as the errant marbles of defecation. Due south and under several rows of seats.

Mortified, the mom stuck her head under her seat, craning her neck to see where on earth the poop had gone. Under someone's feet? Stuck to a purse or a pant leg? Several scenarios presented themselves in her imagination, none of them with happy endings. If she alerted a flight attendant to the situation, there could be chaos, with worried passengers checking their belongings and shoes and whatnot, and all of them giving her dirty looks. Things could get ugly.

So she decided to keep mum about the diaper-changing-session-run-amok, and I can't say as I blame her. The worst that could happen, she reasoned, is that some poor, unsuspecting schlub would get a little poop on his shoe. He probably wouldn't even notice until he got home, and then he could blame it on his neighbor's dog.

The moral of the story is, well, there is no moral per se, but at least you know now that this kind of thing can happen to you, too. At least you've been warned, and maybe you could try to complete all diaper-changing sessions during that window of time when the plane has reached its flying altitude.

There may not be poop rolling next time you and Baby jet somewhere, but trust me, things could get a little stressful anyway. I flew home to Winnipeg often during Jonah's first year; my trips became less frequent during Ezra's babyhood. I found that trips became much more complicated and wild when my boys reached the age of mobility. When they could crawl, and stand, and squirm like octopuses, and when they napped less often, those little frequent flyers morphed into Energizer bunnies.

Gone were the flights of my kid-free days, when I could actually sip a drink and flip through an in-flight magazine. *Avec bébé,* I was on full alert, dispensing bottles, sippy cups, and crackers, and trying to keep a very active boy from stepping or puking on my seatmate's business suit. Both tots loved to peek through the seats and try to engage whoever was back there in some babbling games. Depending on the passenger, this adorable little socializing attempt didn't always fly, which meant I had to wrench my eager beavers away from what they considered great fun and try my best to distract them with books or toys or shredded paper. (Those in-flight mags? Perfect for ripping!)

A few tips I learned the hard way (next page):

 **Discipline Preview**

Before we get to the deeper discipline issues in Month Ten, consider this expert's observation about paving the way via positive attention:

"Disciplining a 7- to 9-month-old probably won't have much effect or make much of a difference in her behavior—and it's usually unnecessary, as babies this young aren't really capable of manipulation or consciously 'being bad.' But you can already start getting in the habit of using techniques that will work. For example, pay a lot of attention to your child when she's playing nicely or lying on her back looking around the room. That way when she's older, you'll already be used to paying attention to her before she misbehaves instead of trying to figure out how to punish her afterward. You can enhance the effectiveness of almost any disciplinary procedure—such as a brief time-out—by making the time when your child is not misbehaving more enjoyable (or, as I call it, 'enhanced time-in')."[3]

—Edward R. Christophersen, Ph.D.

## Behind the Bulkhead

When booking a flight, ask for the bulkhead seats, those immediately behind first class. There is much more room for wiggling, flailing, and maybe even diaper changing. My friend Nancy's baby, Eva, actually napped on the floor in front of her parents' bulkhead seats. If the airline reserves those seats for handicapped people, be early for check-in so you can nab the leftovers (people with kids usually get second dibs).

## Baby's Own Seat

Experts recommend buying a seat for your baby so he can be safely tucked in his car seat in the event of turbulence. Look into the possibility of half-price baby fares.

## Boarding First?

Boarding first, a privilege extended to passengers with little ones, is a mixed blessing. In fact, I like to be about the last person to board to minimize at all costs the dreaded sitting time. Mobile babies and toddlers can zoom around the gate area and blow off extra steam before boarding.

## Folding Umbrella Strollers

For layovers, bring a folding umbrella stroller with a basket underneath for the diaper bag. (Most airlines require heftier strollers to be checked as luggage.) Some nice airline employee will fold up your little stroller and store it somewhere for the flight, and the blessed contraption will appear again when you exit the airplane (that is, just when you need it). After wrestling with a turbo baby for two hours, free arms make you feel like a million frequent flyer miles.

## Help for Changing Pressure

Nursing, a bottle, or pacifier-sucking will protect Baby's ears as the air pressure changes. If your little guy has had a recent ear infection, ask your doc about recommending a decongestant for the flight.

My friend Margaret has logged oodles of air miles shuttling herself and her two bambinos back and forth from Michigan to New Jersey, where she grew up. She's a seasoned pro at this flying-with-tots business, and she has a great tip for you: "Bring an extra set of clothes! You can always grab a snack or makeshift a diaper, but no matter how hard you try, the smell of baby vomit will not come out of your child's or your clothes! When flying

 **Voices**

"I must admit I've never been on a train with my baby. It's just never come up as an option. But if you have, do drop me an e-mail and let me know how it went! Oh, wait! This just in from Lisa H., a friend and brave woman indeed!

"When our oldest daughter, Alexandra, was exactly one year old, we took a train trip from Chicago to Phoenix to spend Christmas with a close relative. We opted not to get a 'sleeper car' due both to the cost and to our belief that we could easily rough it for thirty hours in the large seats. Unfortunately, we forgot to pack baby Tylenol, and Alexandra began screaming just when our fellow passengers were settling into a deep sleep. The train was crowded, and the only place to go to avoid the angry stares of passengers was the lower, cargo level of the train. Bob and I took turns with a screaming baby, who slept only minutes at a time that long, long night. We later found out that she had a double ear infection. The two things we learned: (1) come prepared with the appropriate painkiller, and (2) attend to any budding health problems (that is, take the time for a trip to the pediatrician) before setting out on an adventure like this, especially when you have no control over the driving. Incidentally, we haven't ridden a train since."

I always carry extra outfits for the baby and an extra shirt for me. (Although you will be surprised how fast that seat in the middle of the row opens up for you when your baby does puke!)"

And then we have the Road Trip, a true family bonding classic from time immemorial. In the case of babies, though, the rules change slightly. Instead of breaking up fights in the backseat ("Don't make me stop this car!"), you yourself may well be in the backseat, providing face time for the bored little babe. Even if your tot isn't mobile yet, stop every two hours or so to give Baby some stretching time out of the car seat. A change of scenery, some fresh air, a snack, and a new diaper will do wonders for your tiny traveler's state of mind.

Deborah Geigis Berry, perhaps the queen of traveling with kids (she wrote a book on the topic, and has roamed the free world with her daughter, Cady), offers this savvy hint: "Don't drive all day and put the baby directly into bed. She's too wound up and won't sleep (neither will you)." Geigis Berry suggests taking a warm bath together to relax, following as closely as possible your bedtime ritual from home. The *Goodnight Moon* video, with soothing lullabies, worked wonders with Cady, she said.[4]

Also, the travel guru says, if your baby is accustomed to drifting off to dreamland in her own room, offer her her own space by sitting outside the hotel room door while she falls asleep. Better yet—and this is a tip with a capital *T*—read a magazine in the bathtub (what a concept). As for your husband, he can either take a walk or join you in the bathroom, reading his own magazine, or watch you read yours. It could be good for your love life!

## You Can Dress 'Em Up, but Can You Take Them Anywhere?

One of the most fun aspects of my gig as a freelance entertainment reporter is that I sometimes get to haul the kiddies with me to various restaurants. "Dining Out with Kids" is one of the *Grand Rapids Press*'s most popular columns and a wonderful opportunity for me and the other stringers-with-kids to display for the public our children chewing and sipping—or, if things don't quite work out as planned, spitting up and gagging.

## To Madagascar or Moline: Essentials for Your Carry On

- Ziploc baggies for dirty diapers, leaky bottles, stained tees, and so on.
- Wipes for multiple uses, including to swab faces, hands, clothes, and teething toys that have fallen on the ground.
- Diapers (duh!)
- Bottles of powdered formula. You can add bottled water before you get on board, or if you have a long flight, bring cans of ready-made formula to pour into a clean bottle. (Babies tend to fling bottles on the floor, so have a couple extras just in case.)
- New and exciting toys to distract Baby.
- Age-appropriate snacks, such as Cheerios, crackers, and cereal bars.
- Baby acetaminophen, just in case. If flying, ask your doctor about using a decongestant to relieve pressure and potential pain in Baby's ears.
- An extra outfit for Baby and possibly an extra top for you, too (see Margaret's tip on page 155).
- Have your identification (passport, green card, birth certificate, license, and so on) and Baby's passport or birth certificate bundled together so the nice INS official can quickly skim everything at once. Keep these easily accessible in a plastic I.D. packet that can be worn around your neck, or use a slim travel pouch that can be worn around your waist (typically under the waistband of your pants).

This column, a snapshot of one family's dining experience, is exactly that, an experience, especially when babies and toddlers are involved and the word "shhh" is the extent of your dinner conversation. My job is to check out various eateries around town and evaluate them on their kid-friendly quotient. This has taught me a number of things about dining out with kids. Babies, especially older babies, can be the toughest customers. Of course, teeny little guys can just doze in their carriers while you and your mate/mom/pal happily eat and enjoy stimulating conversation. But when they get mobile and their idea of fun is not—thank you—being crammed into a highchair while there is obviously lots of fascinating stuff on the floor to check out, it gets trickier. Here are some of my formula-for-success tips for lunching with the babe:

### Crackers for Crunching

Ask for crackers first thing. Unless you are super organized and keep a stash of crackers or Cheerios in a cute little container in your diaper bag, you need a munchie for the munchkin—pronto. If you often forget, like me, don't sweat it; this is a dining establishment and they should have crackers, for Pete's sake. So when Tiffany the server girl takes your drink order, ask for crackers. They do a great job of occupying Baby's mouth while you wait for food to come. (Now's a good time to ask your waitress if she would warm up a bottle for you. Many times, they are happy to do this little thing for you, especially if you're nice.)

### Portable Highchair?

If you're a germ freak like my brother, by all means haul along a portable highchair with you everywhere you go. If you're just an attentive parent who would like to—if possible—shield your baby from the cold bug du jour, forget the cumbersome furniture assembly. Just ask for a highchair and slap one of those disposable plastic table topper things on the tray. Even easier: Swab the whole surface area with an antibacterial disposable wipe.

## Finger Food Friendlies

If Baby is used to eating finger foods, order him a bagel, English muffin, or something he's familiar with, tear it into bite-sized pieces, and let him chow down happily. Augment his meal with bites of your mashed potatoes, veggies, and chicken.

## Serious Tipping

Tip at least 20 percent, since Tiffany and Co. are likely to clean up plenty of mashed-in foodstuffs and cracker crumbs from the floor. If she (or he) brought you wet wipes, unasked for, and are friendly to your baby, definitely leave a good tip as a reward.

# On the Relationship Seat: Long-Distance Grandparents

My parents live one thousand miles away from my little family in Grand Rapids, but they've always had a close relationship with my boys. While it's more work to keep these bonds strong than if the grandparents live close by, the rewards of making the effort will last Baby's lifetime. If you want your parents and Baby to be as "tight" as possible, consider these ideas that our family (and others) have used to make it happen.

## Lots of Visits

During the first year of Baby's life, before he gets the hang of the phone and e-mail, try to visit his grandparents as much as you can. Babies under age two fly free with your paid airplane seat; take advantage of the savings while you can. Invite your parents or in-laws to come to your place for vacation this year. When you do get to spend time together, stay in the same house. Strong bonds tend to form after a week of togetherness! Little ones innately know who loves them, and even if the face is a little fuzzy—"Do I know you?"—the genuine affection coming from Grandma and Grandpa speeds up the connection process.

## Photo Album for Baby

Show your baby pictures of his grandparents and talk about them regularly. Put their pictures in a vinyl photo album designed for babies to play with (and gnaw on) or attach a baby-safe photo accessory to Baby's bouncer, swing, play mat (which often include slots for pictures), or infant carrier.

## Video Updates

Invest in a camcorder or occasionally borrow one from a friend. Not only does video make for powerful between-visit updates, but they'll provide a fun record of your child's growth. (Michelle's daughter Casey, now four, often asks to watch videos of "when I was little" rather than the usual Disney fare.) Make sure Grandma and Grandpa are in the video during times when you're together.

## Breaking News

Supply the info-hungry grandparents with lots of photos, e-mails, faxes, postcards, and letters with the latest-breaking news. Alexis got in the habit of sending off "Hall of Momentous Occasions" e-mails to her parents, who loved these quick news flashes about Baby Jessie's first smile, first steps, first playmates, and so on. Alexis made sure to keep the stories brief, fun, and frequent. "Don't feel like you have to write a novel for your parents to appreciate the stories' value," she advises. As with videos, these written records of your child's growth will provide a fun record for the future. You might even suggest that your parents keep copies in a notebook to give back to your child someday.

## Postcards for Baby

Jacob's grandparents, who travel internationally, began sending him postcards from places they visited as soon as he was old enough to look at the pictures. Their notes on the back told Jacob fun facts about the pictures, which were usually of traditional cultural costumes, native children, and animals who live in these different regions. His mom laminated the cards with clear contact paper and kept them in a box for him to look through whenever he wanted. Even stateside grandparents can do something similar with postcards from their hometown.

## Make a Recording

Send your parents a few blank cassettes and a list of your child's favorite picture books. Grandparents can borrow the books from their local library and record themselves reading the stories, complete with turn-the-page "dings," sound effects, and funny voices. (Grandparents who like to buy books as gifts can make their presents extra special by recording their storytelling.) This is a fun way for Baby to grow familiar with Grandma and Grandpa's voices when they're still too young for extended phone conversations.

Dearest Shulamit,

As quick as a breeze through the trees, you are not far from turning one. It's been a busy, exciting, and eventful first year. My heart is filled with love for you and your sisters, Aliza, Ariela, and Elisheva.

Our lives are secure and protected by the shield of unrelenting love from your father. One of the most special gifts he has given you is his example of what a good man is. He is filled with spirit, sacrifice, and tenderness. Each Friday night, in the glow of the Sabbath candles, he places his hands on your head and, in a hushed voice, whispers in Hebrew to G-d: "May G-d make you like Sarah, Rebecca, Rachel, and Leah. May G-d bless you and safeguard you. May G-d illuminate His countenance for you and be gracious to you. May G-d turn His countenance to you and establish peace for you. Let them place My Name upon the Children of Israel, and I shall bless them."

Shuli, when Daddy and I chose a name for you, we thought it would be so hard to find one that suited you and defined you. You came to us, as G-d destined it since the time of creation, and once you were in our arms, it was as simple as if someone had whispered your name in our ears. Shulamit Bracha, a blessing of completeness, of perfection.

You are a marvel, little one, as uncomplicated as daylight and just as wondrous. As you see the world for the first time, so do I. When you laugh and delight your sisters with your fun-loving nature, I recognize how blessed I am. As I imagine each of you as women, a sense of ease washes over me, for I know that my daughters are equipped with the values and self-worth that will carry them well into adulthood. I look forward to the day when I kiss you under the chuppah [Jewish wedding canopy] and send you into a life as filled with blessings as my life is. That is my wish for you and your sisters: happiness, love, Torah, and sanctuary in your own family.

All my love,

Your mother, Aviva

—Aviva Cohen, mother of Aliza, Ariela, Elisheva,
and Shulamit

# Disciplining Dish,
# Childproofing Chatter,
# and Enduring Tough In-Laws

*Milemarker!* "Bamalama!" Is there some way your child could have learned Finnish behind your back? Because he's definitely not speaking English. Oh, maybe a few words are noticeable—"Mama," "Dada," "bye-bye"—but on the whole, Baby's conversation is indecipherable. His sounds are indeed becoming more and more like a language, however, a lilting, almost musical form of expression that is absolutely precious. Baby does understand the meaning of a few words: When prompted, "Show me," he can point to a fair number of objects, especially those that hold special meaning in his universe.

## Now We're Cruising

The world is your baby's oyster, and she will dream up oodles of ways to check out all its bells and whistles via standing, speed crawling, and maybe even climbing. At this special phase of a baby's life, I have one word for you: babyproof, babyproof, babyproof. Because your first, budding attempts at discipline are so connected to protecting Baby from harm, childproofing is a biggie right now. In some ways, they go hand-in-hand. So I consulted with a panel of young moms to discuss both issues, and their tips and ideas are woven throughout this chapter. It's not as complicated or mysterious as you might be led to believe, and a few plug covers and gates (Poison Control on the speed dial might not be a bad idea either) will mean you can let Busy Baby roam freely about his universe.

Still, "you can only do so much rearranging, unplugging, fencing off, and locking up and still have your house retain the semblance of a human habitat. Baby will simply have to learn there will always be a few areas that remain off limits."[1] *Easier said than done,* you wryly observe.

Take the toilet, for example. A toilet has the power to transfix a baby, and cordoning it off isn't exactly practical. Given half a chance, the mite would be glued to the commode, watching in utter fascination as he swishes, dunks, and otherwise baptizes in it whatever object he can find. (Incidentally, it matters not to Baby if the toilet has been flushed. This trick he has picked up from the dog, which now snores innocently by the space heater in the hall). My Ez would *sprint* to the toilet if he thought he had an iota of a chance to glimpse a "swirly" or get a look-see at the ever-fascinating depths within. Hopefully his early interest in the toilet is a good sign, like maybe he will become one of those potty training phenoms that supposedly run in the family. One can always hope. Get one of those toilet seat–latch doohickeys, which prevent Mr. Splash-o-Rama from deep-sixing his rubber ducky, your watch, and other household items. Of course, you don't want your baby's chubby little hands to host a bacteria convention either.

Each ten-month-old baby will surprise her parents with different breakthroughs in motor development. Don't compare your little one's crawling with your sister's kid's cruising. Every baby takes a slightly different path to mobility. She may be crawling around at a good clip or still kind of scooting. She might be climbing, and she may or may not have a clue as to how to climb down. Some babes are traversing the room about now, clinging to furniture, and a few overachievers have even been known to walk at this point, although I suspect their parents are goading them on with an electric prod or something. At the very minimum, your baby should have aced sitting by now. Turning, leaning, and changing positions should be a piece of cake. If your tyke is still kind of lounging around while her play-date pals loop around her, don't sweat it. I'm serious! Count your blessings for a laid-back baby; there is time enough for her to become interested in moving around more. Because when she walks, she can get into way more stuff, see? And that's when the fun really starts.

If your baby is one of those turbocharged types, you'll find yourself facing unique joys and challenges. For one thing, she may be so stoked about her new motor activities that she loses sleep over it. And when she loses sleep, you lose sleep, remember? I hate to tell you this, but all of your child's physical activity may not translate into more sleep. These days, Baby may have already decided that two naps a day are for little kids, not her. She may only snooze about eleven hours a night, with a one-hour nap. Lots of babies, when they wake up for whatever reason, decide to pop up and try out the nifty little trick of standing. *Sleep, schmeep!* they think. *Who has time for shuteye when I can stand?* Clutching the crib rails, the narcoleptic little nub will go for it, rocking and rolling and generally causing a hubbub in the household. Don't worry: This too shall pass.

Also, in the midst of all the excitement the bouncing babe feels about doing new stuff, she may need more help from you making the shift from activity to slumber. Just before bedtime, hold her in your lap, perhaps in a rocking chair, while she has her evening bottle or while you look at a chunky board book together. With my rambunctious babies, it helped to just move the party into their bedroom about half an hour before sleep. Then I would change their diapers and put them in soft pajamas, getting them primed for a more relaxed pace. The hoped-for result was to get Baby in bed, still awake but calm (at least calmer than an hour before, when full-tilt wrecking-ball activities raged).

A bedtime story is wonderful, even if your baby—like mine—is more interested in pulling books off the shelves than following the story. Ez was good for about thirty seconds during this phase, depending on how zonked he was, and then he would cut loose and crawl off my lap. Still, I always tried to finish the story, reading out loud until the book was done even if he seemed oblivious. Once in a while he would pause and listen, or

 **Voices**

"The best advice I have heard and adhered to as a parent in regard to the safety of a growing baby/toddler is if you don't want him to touch it, climb on it, or play with it, then you must remove it. At first this can seem as though Junior has just conquered another part of your life. But in the long run, it saves you money: Not as many things get broken, and you don't have to purchase as many throat drops to soothe your throat because you're yelling NO! all the time.

"In our house we began with all the normal 'redecorating,' like installing outlet covers and locks for cabinets and drawers. We put all medicines, cleaning products, and toxic substances way up on top shelves to keep them out of reach. We also found ourselves attaching bookcases and dressers to the walls, installing permanent swing gates, and climbing over removable gates.

"Another challenge for us was trying to keep our climbers from getting on top of the dining room table. We found two solutions: Initially we began using folding chairs—not so the chair would collapse and catch the culprit in the act, but so we could fold them up and put them away and have no chairs around the table unless we were sitting in them. A later solution we came to was that if we used heavy enough chairs around the table, the child couldn't move them out to climb on. We tried using picnic tablecloth clips to keep tablecloths from being pulled down, and we removed anything on the tablecloth. When the clips broke, we got rid of tablecloths and went to place mats.

maybe even grab the book and flip a few pages. He was soothed by the soft cadence of my voice, and the singsong quality of stories like *Goodnight Moon.* Experts say reading to your baby is one way of boosting her love of language. It's also so cozy, sweet, and, well, I liked to look at the pictures even if he didn't!

"Christmas was always challenging. How do you keep the Christmas tree from falling on top of the curious child who just can't resist all those pretty ornaments? We came up with the perfect solution, at least for those who have artificial trees. Our tree has three sections, so we just used the top two sections to create a mini-Christmas tree, which we placed on top of our piano. Ta-dah! We could have our Christmas tree and keep the baby safe too.

"At times we have done all in our power to keep our children safe, but it hasn't worked. We used to have a TV/playroom upstairs. On afternoons when I taught piano lessons, a baby-sitter would come in and play with all the kids up there. At the top of the stairs, a swing gate was attached permanently to the wall. I always insisted that the gate be locked. Well, one day during my piano lesson I began to hear this thump, thump, cry, cry, thump, thump, cry, cry. I found my nine-month-old child rolling down the steps one by one. I looked up to the top of the stairs and saw that the gate was still locked. How could this little child of mine scale the gate? Who knows? I admit I questioned the baby-sitter as to whether he had gotten tired of her and stuck her over the gate to fend for herself. He assured me he hadn't.

"Well, I know there were times we resorted to yelling NO! but as often as we could we tried to take care of the problem before it occurred."

—Dawn

# Achtung, Baby!

Don't be suckered by that cute, blank look on Junior's face. He's now wise to the word *no,* and he may even repeat it and shake his head. Saying no does not dissuade him, however. Inexhaustible in his quest for thrills, he charges from one danger zone to the next even though you've consistently told him no. (It will take several more months for Baby to nod his head and say yes.)

Teaching your baby self-control is not easy, and it calls for more patience than you or I probably currently have. Praying for this virtue becomes a must. You especially need to get a grip on things or scenarios that pose danger to your baby. Above all, she needs to get on a cellular level that some issues are simply not up for discussion.

Baby will definitely be more obliging when the matter at hand is somehow advantageous to him. Like if he holds his spoon during lunch, for instance, instead of flinging it at you, he will get chow. Or if he sits down in the tub, nicelike, Daddy could very possibly sing a verse or two of "Rubber Ducky" in that Huey, Duey, and Louie voice that just busts Baby up every time. Let's say, though, that the proposed activity holds no appeal. Like, none. Zero. Zilch.

*Let me see if I actually comprehend what you're saying to me, Mom: You want me, the man-child who puts the* ram *in rambunctious, the* boy *in bois- terous, to be still while you change my pants? Let me see if we're on the same page here: Stone-still? Motionless? Quiescent? Uh, no. Not interested. No thanks. Get back to me in about eighty years, when I actually feel like sitting around like a veal.*

And when he goes postal on you, screaming blue murder, arching his back, flipping stubbornly from side to side as you develop your triceps and force him to lie in one position, you realize there's another, rather balky side to your baby. As you pin him down with one arm and try desperately to swab at a moving target with wipes (and at this point poop is smeared on your hands, his feet, his clean sweatpants, your watch), your voice starts to get louder. But when the Great Twenty-Pound Escape Artist realizes his darling mommy is actually kind of (let's admit it) *yelling* at him, his flailing limbs go limp, his bottom lip juts out, and he falls apart in disgrace. Then of course you feel bad for losing your cool, you vow to remain calm during the next diaper change, you wonder why you are such a terrible mother, your own bottom lip juts out, and so it goes. I averted some of the chaos by keeping a box of crackers on the changing table, and my guys began to expect a little snack at changing time. They were much more agreeable and managed to help me keep the poop contained. Better Parenting Through Bribery? Hey, whatever works.

## Discipline: The First Frontier

So here you are, at one of the biggest intersections of your parenting trip: discipline. What a loaded word! It makes some of you cringe, the thought of punishing your precious baby simply too painful to bear. Others, though, in search of wisdom on an extremely important subject, may perk up at the word. For me, one of the concepts of parenting hardest to embrace has been that it's entirely up to Doyle and me to lead our boys away from the bad and toward the good. But of course babies, being possessed of original sin and predisposed to get themselves into heaps of messy situations, have already shown you in numerous ways that they need direction. "Man is born to trouble as surely as sparks fly upward," the Good Book says (Job 5:7). And just like a little piece of ash, fluttering around helplessly in the wind and about to be carried off to who knows where, your baby will, at times, go one way or another. You need to help him go the right way and not fly off, uncontrolled and aimless, to follow whatever whim blows into his life.

In my thesaurus, some of the synonyms for *discipline* have a negative connotation: *punishment, bite the bullet, castigation.* Whoa! If you're anything like me, the thought of "castigating" my beautiful baby, no matter how many times he's poked his sticky fingers in the VCR, is way too much. But some of the meanings for discipline are decidedly positive: "correction," "self-regulate," "train." And when you consider the alternative (antonyms for discipline: *laziness, sloth, slip, neglect*), the apparent need for healthy discipline becomes fairly sobering.

We've got to help our babies learn and develop by offering love-bound limits, and the time to start is now. *Why so soon?* some of you with angelic, calm, probably immobile babies are wondering. Well, between a ten-month-old's zeal for exploration, magnetic attraction to anything dangerous, and his short—but present—memory, lots of situations have/will come up where some corrective measures have been/will be useful.

 **Voices**

"We tried to keep Kid #1 from the CDs by over and over lifting her away and saying in her face, 'No! No CDs.' Two months later, exhausted, we moved anything she shouldn't touch out of reach. And don't trust the 'childproof' door latches. If kids just yank the doors hard enough, they'll open. Move everything above reach!"

—Lisa

"We started 'training' Bethany two months ago by saying no and looking sternly at her. If she goes back to the certain activity again, she gets another no. If she goes back again, she gets a flick on the head. If she does it again, she gets flicked again, and that usually ends it for that episode at least. She is now, at ten months old, pretty good at not touching the Christmas tree or approaching stairs. We have also used this approach for the stereo, fireplace, and spitting food."

—Meredith

Even at this preverbal stage (unless of course your baby is a talking prodigy), experts urge parents to start drawing and maintaining borders and boundaries. There are different ways of doing this, of course, but some limits are crucial to establishing the fact that you, not him, make the rules and decide big things. After all, there are definitely bigger fish to fry in the future. It's like that old saying, "Cook 'em while they're minnows and they won't stink up the place when they're big ol' fat catfish." (Or did I just make that up?)

When you stick to your guns about a few key matters, you send an important message. "Will [Baby] understand what you are saying? Probably not at first, but she will pick up on your reaction to what she is doing. More important, her amazing little computer is continually

> "We started disciplining as soon as possible, primarily with behaviors that had potential to cause our daughter harm. We didn't want to say no constantly and so said 'danger!' instead. It helped her (and us) sort out the dangerous (what we wanted her to have sense to avoid) and the inconvenient (things we needed to take care of for her, such as keeping breakables out of reach). We'd simply remove the source (or remove her from it) if the message didn't get across."
>
> —Erin

> "We clashed—and still clash—very much on discipline. My husband is much stricter than I am, and we have had our share of scraps about many, many, many, many things. We are still working on resolving and meeting in the middle. My philosophy is if she's not in danger and she might learn something, then discipline is okay. My husband's philosophy is if her behavior gets on his nerves, then she should stop it. You can clearly see that we've got issues here."
>
> —Laura

processing information about 'what happens when I ———?' And you definitely want to provide a lot of the input."[2]

Some moms, like my friend Meredith, put a good-for-them spin on discipline. Instead of shirking from her duties as a disciplinarian, she and her husband both view this process as a wonderful act of care and love. (Indeed, sometimes it will be much easier to say yes than to say no, like when your toddler is screaming like a banshee in Piggly Wiggly and you know a lollipop would make your life infinitely more pleasant.) "Chad and I love training (not discipline)," says Meredith. "We find that it is fun and effective."

Call it "training" if that seems less harsh, but start doing it the next time Baby heads for that lamp with a wicked gleam in her eye. The point is not to be mean or to lash out in the heat of the moment, but to actually start to change her course of action. It's for her benefit and safety, now and when she's eighty, and it will make your job of parenting easier in the long run too. "Little ones," says writer Paula Spencer, "are as much in need as older children of being kept safe from harm and of developing a sense of security that will fuel their explorations and discoveries."[3]

One last thing about beginning to discipline your baby: It's a great idea to always "accentuate the positive," in life and in raising babies. A wonderful idea I grabbed hold of when Jonah was about eighteen months—and driving me up the wall with his constant negativity (which is perfectly normal for this age, but still irritating)—was to intentionally delight in his good behavior long before having to deal with the bad.

## Oh, Behave!

Many newbie parents I've talked to have griped about the word *no* losing its meaning—and fast. Some, like Erin, save the word for special occasions, like when the little bug is about to eat, well, a little bug, or stick her fingers in a fan, or guzzle suntan lotion (which my son attempted three days ago)!

I've heard of people—mostly from our parents' generation—who felt so strongly that "no" should suffice that they didn't bother with latches, gates, or fancy childproofing. Now that I've been through this stage with my wild and woolly guys, I have to conclude that if this system works for you, you have an extraordinarily compliant, eager-to-please Baby. Jonah and Ez were both extremely curious and active, and I'm sure I would have been in a rest home by now if I hadn't outfitted the house with every preventive device known to humankind.

Here's the thing: Babies are not out to defy you when they ignore your no. An unwavering desire to explore, taste, grab, chew, and throw is normal, and Baby's determination to investigate should not be viewed as the first step toward a life of crime. She may scoot toward the CD rack ten times, not because she is trying to take charge but because it looks utterly fascinating, and her attention span is short.

At this age, though, she does have some memory stored in that ever-expanding, exploding-with-information brain of hers. So it is time to get firm with whatever limits you plan to set. "Baby not only understands what you're saying, but has enough memory to recall that you got mad when he did something previously. Of course, he can also remember that last night when he cried in the middle of the night, you picked him up and rocked him. Or brought him into your bed. Or if he cried long enough for something—say a bottle in bed—you gave in. So be careful about falling into habits that may be tougher now to break."[4]

Babies do know what *no* means, even if the oomph of the word loses something after about eight thousand repeats. When approaching the forbidden staircase (or toilet, or oh-so-chewable dog toys, or Grandma Pat's Hummel figurines), Ez would turn to me (or whomever) and, if we caught his eye, shake his head solemnly. Depending on how enticing the *verboten* object or climbing apparatus was, he either stopped in his tracks at "No, no!" or continued on with mischief making, content in the knowledge that he had time for one good climb/swish/chew/smash before some big person removed him.

# On the Relationship Seat: Of In-Laws and Outlaws

Kelly knew her mother-in-law might be a bit of a handful when her baby, Baxter, arrived, but she never imagined just how intrusive and critical

---

 **Voices**

"This is how we childproof every morning: Elevate all the garbage cans, close the bedroom and bathroom doors, barricade all the plug outlets so Bennett can't unplug anything (the others have plug covers), scan the floor from his angle to try spotting the off-limits items before he does, and—the inevitable—continually remove him from everything. But he thinks it's so great to be where he's not supposed to be. He knows the bathroom is off limits. (Fun! We might not have emptied Max's potty yet!) It seems he has his radar tuned to when that door is open, even when he can't see it. He must sense it! It's actually quite amusing because the race is on: Who can get there first? Bennett or one of the rest of us? And Max is always hollering, 'Bennett's going to the bathrooooooom!' "

—Alanna

"Emma actually crawled into the bathroom and put one of those toilet screw covers in her mouth and choked on it. Disgusting *and* scary. My solution: Take off the covers since there's no way to attach them. That became our entire method."

—Lisa

"Strangely enough, we never childproofed our house that much. Amelia just wasn't interested in sticking forks into outlets or chewing on extension cords. We did use the outlet blocks though, and the cupboard locks on the dangerous cupboards. We also made a kid's

Grandma Poolstra would actually become. "Everything I did was wrong, from not putting an undershirt on the baby—in ninety-degree heat!—to not bathing him enough to 'spoiling' Baxter by breast-feeding him on demand," Kelly laments. "I tried to graciously handle her comments, but when she told me one day I was 'letting myself go' by not losing weight

cupboard full of safe and interesting kitchen things that she could freely play with. That way she felt like she was delving into forbidden cupboards when in reality they were completely safe.

From a very early age, Amelia understood the word 'dangerous,' and it was very effective when said in a low tone. She understood the tone of my voice more than anything and was always good to stay away from things if I told her why they were dangerous. She never even really went through much of a climbing-on-the-wall-unit stage either, despite the fact that she is a bit of a daredevil. It helped to make sure there were always exciting but controlled things going on in her life (such as having Daddy swing her around by the feet in the yard, holding hands and jumping off the steps, and so on)."

—Laura

"Don't childproof too early. Tim and I spent a bundle on cupboard locks and had the house entirely proofed before we brought our daughter home from the hospital. By the time she was old enough to get into anything, we'd broken all those little plastic things opening and closing them several times a day. Sheesh. Our A-Number-One investment was two stairway gates, one for the top and one for the bottom. We continue to use those even now that she's four, especially to keep her from wandering down the dark staircase at night while the rest of us sleep."

—Erin

faster, I lost it." Her temper, that is. Kelly's not alone in her chagrin: Many new parents are shocked at the criticisms and unsolicited tips sent their way by everyone, but mainly by their respective sets of parents. When you embark on parenthood, nothing prepares you for the fact that you're a bull's-eye for the infant dogma of one and all on how to raise Baby "right" (a.k.a.: their way).

Ellen experiences ongoing jabs from her own mother as she and her husband care for Abby and Eliza. "I know she's just trying to be helpful, but when she rolls her eyes at Eliza's pacifier or makes these none-too-subtle remarks about my part-time job, it really undermines my confidence as a mother."

Mixing up the pot even more is the fact that you can't easily blow off the comments of your parents or in-laws the same way you might a stranger's two cents. You're stuck with these people every Thanksgiving—at least—for years to come. Also, it behooves you to at least try to maintain some kind of positive relationship with the grandparents, if not for your sake then for your child's.

Easier said than done, my friend Karen might say. Listen to her story:

> It all started the minute Bryan and I got engaged: My future mother-in-law informed me that she wouldn't attend our wedding if we chose to dance. We had been engaged for two weeks when we made the trip to their home, and that conversation about the dancing happened within two hours of my arrival. Our relationship has gone downhill ever since.
>
> She waltzes into my home about twice a year and, even though she doesn't live with or care for my children on a daily basis, thinks she understands their feeding habits, their sleeping patterns, and the best ways to discipline them. I'm in the bonding and attachment camp. We don't choose to schedule our kids. It works for us

and for our children, but she believes we're creating an environ-
ment for failure, self-indulgence, and lack of structure. Nothing
could be further from the truth. The hardest part is her assumption
that I haven't thought about what would be best for *my* kids. She
doesn't trust my instincts, doesn't value my investment in things
foreign to her (like long-term breast-feeding), and believes that I'm
actually harming my kids. The truth is that my kids are happy,
adjusted, nurtured children with a great sense of self. They lead
rather disciplined, love-filled lives.

She even goes so far as to correct me in front of my kids when
I don't do things "right." My four-year-old is starting to understand
that Mommy and Grandma don't agree on most things and that
Grandma has a piece of advice or a reason for everything. What a
confusing message for a kid—and, truthfully, not one that endears
him to his grandmother.

In the beginning, I blamed Bryan for his mother's behavior
and expected him to somehow remedy her. At times I wanted out
of the marriage just to get away from her—crazy talk, but I wanted
an escape. I am grateful that Bryan sees his mother for who she
really is—a broken, self-loathing individual without many sources
of love in her life. We're a team on this one. My husband once
wrote his parents a two-page letter detailing the boundaries of our
relationship with them—what's acceptable, what isn't, and the con-
sequences associated with those actions. *He* enforces the boundaries
so I don't have to shoulder that alone. Also, his loyalty has always
been and will always be with me. It's taken almost seven years to
get to a place where I feel protected from her, but we're in a good
place now. His mother hasn't changed, but we've changed our attitude about her and have worked really hard to establish boundaries
in the relationship.

I've resigned myself to the fact that she may never change, but that's not my problem. I'm not responsible for her life; I'm responsible for my life and my family and my attitude toward her. When I reprimand her for trying to take over, I remind her of the boundaries we've set as a family. She doesn't like it, but she accepts it.

Unfortunately, she gets her self-worth from putting other people down. The *real* problem is that she's terribly insecure. Lashing out at me and my parenting skills is her way of elevating herself. I don't like it when she tears me down, but at least now I've come to understand what motivates her. It's not about me or my kids; it's about her and her feelings of inadequacy and loneliness.

Bryan and I have done our best to shield our kids from our true feelings about their grandmother. We want her to be successful with our kids; however, she's doing a mighty fine job of wrecking it herself when she chooses to tear us down in front of them. Our kids adore us, and they're always going to choose us over her. No kid likes somebody who flagrantly disrespects their parent.

Karen's experience illustrates a key need in weathering these worst-case scenarios: Do all you can to separate yourself from the things your parents and parents-in-law are responsible for themselves. Turn your eyes toward the responsibilities that *you* should attend to—like right responses, healthy boundaries, and gracious attitudes—rather than remain focused on the infuriating behaviors you can't control.

Tact is in order, lots and lots of it. A sense of humor, if you can muster it, wouldn't hurt either. A lighthearted deflection of a zinger—"Don't worry about me feeding Sasha formula, Mom. After all, you fed me evaporated milk and look how I thinned out!"—can smooth over a ruffled moment like nothing else. Remember the Good Book's guidance on this: "A gentle answer turns away wrath" (Proverbs 15:1).

Try to remember too that the new granny's (or grandpa's) comments are probably well-meaning and that they spring from a need to be recognized and appreciated in her new role. Look for ways you can affirm their contributions without enabling violations of the boundaries you and your spouse want to maintain.

### Quotable

"When you have your first baby and the pacifier falls to the floor, you pick it up and boil it. But when you get to the fourth, you just lick off the pacifier and give it back. You realize that all you need to do is feed 'em, love 'em, and keep 'em out of traffic."

—Michael J. Fox

Ultimately, Baby could be the bridge to a new and stronger relationship with your interfering relatives. After all, you all agree that Baby is gorgeous and brilliant and advanced in every way. Hopefully, as Baby grows and thrives and Mommy-in-Law-Dearest notices you haven't dropped him on his head or accidentally fed him fertilizer, she may calm down and back off. Or, since you and your little family will likely gravitate quite naturally to the friendliest, least critical side of the clan, the faultfinding forebear may get a clue that she better zip it or risk losing a precious relationship.

## Things That Make You Go "Eewww!"

Now that Junior is crawling, cruising, or even walking, every day becomes a Lewis-and-Clark expedition of discovery—and danger. Experts say one surefire way of identifying possible hazards is to crawl around the house yourself. Kind of strange, yes, but this method will prove to be enlightening as on Baby's eye level you get a much better sense of what he sees and could possibly break, swallow, or topple down on himself. Your baby will, I guarantee you, do some things that gross you out beyond your previous capacity to be grossed out. He will most likely nibble on cat food, taste the toilet screw cover (see Lisa's story on page 174), and maybe even imbibe the contents of his own diaper just for sport. The dog is his role model in these disgusting endeavors, so blame her. Keep Poison Control's number handy and remember that a little dirt never hurt anyone.

# The Top Ten Things to Do to Keep Your Home Safe

With the vigilance of a Secret Service agent, attend to the following details in your home:

## 1. Wind Up Cords
Use cord spools and shorteners to wind up dangling electrical and phone cords. Separate and bind up all window-covering cords on window cleats. Use shades instead of blinds in the nursery.

## 2. Cap Outlets
Cap off outlets and use furniture to hide tempting electrical cords.

## 3. Tablecloth Checks
Give a good tug to your tablecloths whenever they're under hot or heavy items. Make sure Baby couldn't pull a steaming dish off the table.

## 4. Dishwasher Dos and Don'ts
Load sharp knives and breakables into the dishwasher when Baby isn't around. (Ez loves to play with the dishwasher, taking things out and putting them back in.)

## 5. Cushion Sharp Edges
Newly walking babies fall like crazy, so invest in a few cushioned edge protectors for your coffee table's sharp corners (or put the coffee table in the garage for a while).

## 6. Barricade Your Garbage

Babies adore garbage. In fact, anything just teeming with bacteria seems to offer no end of tantalization. Anchor your big garbage cans to the wall so Baby can't tip them over, and cover little wastebaskets so he can't dig around and eat paper clips—or worse.

## 7. Put Up Poisonous Houseplants

If you have houseplants on the ground level, make sure they aren't poisonous. I keep poinsettias year-round, not because my thumb is glow-in-the-dark green but because they seem to thrive on coffee and neglect. Keep these and other toxic plants far out of Baby's curious reach—and mouth.

## 8. Lock Up the Dangerous Stuff

Poisonous cleaners, medicines, detergents, and other dangers need to be locked in high cabinets. Even though your baby's no gymnast yet, you definitely want to stay one step ahead of the game on this one.

## 9. Place Tippy Furniture Out of Reach

Lamps, especially the tippy kind, are tempting in the extreme. Arrange your less-sturdy lamps behind heavy pieces of furniture.

## 10. Scan for Small Items

Constantly scan and scour your floor for items small enough to fit into a toilet paper tube. If it's small enough for the roll, it's small enough to choke Baby. For the same reasons, you may have to restrict certain toys. Homemade dolls with buttons and trinkets that Baby can tug off are prime offenders.

---

Always assume your baby is capable of more than you might think. Chances are, she is. The thing that is so hard to accept, for me anyway, is that our most priceless treasures don't come with a warranty; there's just no way to guarantee the absolute safety of our children. Childproof to the best of your ability, but don't go overboard with gimmicky products. You will hear lots of horror stories on television and read about them in the newspapers, about *E. coli* in public pools, listeria in hot dogs, and finger-amputating pack 'n plays. It's up to you to decide how sheltered you want your baby to be. Remember that the odds are good that something unforeseen and unpleasant will probably befall your child despite your best efforts to keep him safe. Not long ago, Doyle was opening the oven and didn't notice Ez crawling behind him. Sure enough, our inquisitive little guy planted both hands on the hot oven door, got burned, and howled in pain for the next two hours. It was miserable to see him hurting like that, but he did in fact learn a pretty hard lesson: "Hot" equals "ouch!"

Your baby's safety is another item on your premium prayer list. Your Father in heaven fashioned her with exquisite care, and He watches and takes care of her. Seeking His wisdom on a daily basis—even for the everyday routines of parenting—will help keep your concerns in perspective and tap into a strength and insight far deeper than your own.

Darling Little Bennett,

You are now eleven months old. I look at you and wonder where the days have gone. You're not a little baby anymore. You are becoming so independent. These days I have to follow you everywhere—you're investigating everything! It is such a joy to see you enjoying your newfound freedom. You have just begun to pull yourself to a standing position, and you are so proud of yourself. You break into this amazing laugh when I acknowledge your accomplishment, and your face is a ray of happy sunshine!

Your hugs are so amazing, Benny. I like this little game we play. I pick you up, hold you above my head, and then lower you. Then you snuggle your face into my neck and you squeal and laugh. When I breast-feed you, you rest your foot up on my shoulder. You're usually barefoot, so I love to kiss your feet. They're so soft and round and so ticklish. I know this sounds silly, but your feet are so expressive! Your little ankles are so busy, setting your feet into circular motion when you are impatient to be fed or picked up, and your chubby little big toe points straight up. I love watching your feet.

You are so happy and laid back, Bennett. You never put up a fuss when Max grabs his toys from you. You just go and find something else to play with—and with purpose and determination. When I hand you to someone with whom I feel comfortable, you just sit there and look at them and have a "Who are you and why are you holding me?" expression on your face. Satisfaction and joy flood my being when I feel your little dimpled hands grabbing my pant legs, wanting to be picked up. I am so thankful that I can be home full-time with you and Max. It is such a privilege to be here whenever you both have a need—physical, emotional, or spiritual. Bennett, Daddy and I are thoroughly enjoying the miracle of life and learning as we watch you develop. We are so thankful that God gave you to us to love and train. We love you just the way you are. God made you exactly how He wanted you to be. I love you, my little treasure, and I always will.

> With so much love,
> Mommy
> —Alanna Friesen, mother of Max and Bennett

# Baby-Sitters, Bye-Byes, and Books, Glorious Books!

*Milemarker!* Whoo-hoo! It's time to party, or at least that's what Baby's thinking. She can pull herself up now, lower herself gracefully into a sitting position (no more plopping for her!), and climb, climb, climb. One day you may catch your sunshine girl doing yoga—or something like it—as she bows deeply at the waist and contemplates all the topsy-turvy stuff in her new universe.

## Tom (Dick and Harry) Cruise

Stash those pricey coffee table books and knickknacks because your baby is about to move along the furniture at a speed that will amaze you. Not only will the Cruisemeister exhibit incredible fleetness of foot on his treks around the living room, but he'll also display an astonishing interest in removing any and all items in his path. Books, magazines, coasters, et al. will go flying. Your floor will soon resemble a hurricane corridor, and you will feel as if you exist for the sole purpose of tidying up after his numerous rampages.

You could just not worry about a few items on the floor, which will make your life infinitely easier. My brother, bless his heart, got the clean gene in the family. Truly, you should see his sock drawer. None of this slipshod jumble of rolled up socks for him. Dan's hosiery is regimented, with the bright whites folded in crisp packets, the ecru giving way to beige, brown, gray, charcoal, black. You get the visual. Now that he's a dad of an eleven-month-old, though, his previously spotless habitat is a tad harder to maintain. As his loving sister, however, I view this passage in my meticulous brother's life from orderly and organized to helpless ball of mush (due to his great love for his daughter, who drools on his carpet, chews on his magazines, and throws up on him) with compassion. And, it must be said for honesty's sake, great, great mirth.

Stairs will become the bane of your existence as your climber risks life and limb to clamber up all the steps she can muster before you catch her. Hopefully, you do catch her because what goes up must come down, and she's still about a month or two away from scaling down.

We were at our wit's end with Ez at this age. If we looked away for a second, the opportunistic little bug would be halfway up the stairs. After seventy rounds of "No, no, Ez. No stairs!" he finally got the message: For some unfathomable reason, we didn't want him to climb the stairs. Then he would look at us and shake his head no, only to proceed to the summit as fast as his chubby little legs could carry him. We tried a few homemade gates to save on the expense of yet another gate (we already had two installed in our house), but Ezra always figured out a way to crawl under the dining room chairs or over other blockades. Finally, we broke down and got an expensive, sturdy gate that has proven to be a key investment in our mental health. The only member of the household who isn't enormously impressed with that gate is Ez. No, not impressed in the least. All that to say, it's time for you to get another gate. Baby will be safer and you will be saner.

## On the Relationship Seat: Get a Life; Get a Sitter

I will never forget the first time I left Jonah. My firstborn was only six weeks old—a little young to leave him with anyone, I thought—but Doyle was a groomsman in his cousin's wedding, and we determined Jonah would be better off with Grandma Pat and Grandpa George, his newly minted surrogate grandparents, than at a fancy wedding. Actually, I think the main reason was that I didn't have any confidence nursing in public—none—and the thought of surreptitiously whipping out a breast while wearing a swanky dress? Uh-uh. Wasn't going to happen. Nope, all things considered, wee Jonah would be much happier at Grandma Pat's, where he would have only to squeak, and the attentive grandparents would stick a bottle in his mouth.

 **Separation Anxiety**

"At this age, most babies have typically already begun to show the signs of separation anxiety. Your baby may start to be shy or anxious around strangers, especially when tired or cranky, and when you're out of sight and not with him, he'll become upset. Although it's hard to see your baby distressed, it's important to let him experience this. When you leave your baby and return, proving that you always come back, you're helping him develop trust and the ability to form attachments to other people.

"When you leave your baby, kiss and hug him and tell him you'll be back. If he's frightened or just falls apart, take the extra time to calm and reassure him. It's hard not to cry when he starts crying, but your breaking down only prolongs the agony. It may help to have someone else he's familiar with (not a new baby-sitter) there to calm him. If your baby gets anxious about nighttime separations, spend some extra cuddle time reading, snuggling, and softly singing together with him before you put him to bed.

"Some babies are good at separations and some aren't—it depends on their temperament. Every child is different, as is the amount of reassurance each needs. If you know your baby needs more calming, don't feel bad about giving it or worry that you're just drawing out the process: You know your child better than anyone else, so follow your instincts."[1]

Dropping him off was utterly wrenching. We weren't yet off the Vanderlaans' driveway when I began to choke up. "Maybe I shouldn't go," I said tearfully. "It's too soon to leave him." Doyle, all gussied up in a tux, viewed me with bewilderment. After all, he had left Jonah plenty of times already, and wasn't the baby thriving?

"He's in great hands," Doyle started in, trying to reassure me.

"I knowwwwww," I blubbered. "But I miss him."

Doyle tried various tactics to get me to see the light, reasoning that the solemn wedding ceremony was no place for a screaming baby. Blah, blah, blah. Finally, he said exactly the wrong thing: "It's not as if we're taking our pet to be euthanized, you know."

Well, needless to say, that remark fell flat. Very flat. Concave, in fact. "How very, very sensitive of you to point out that we are in fact not having our pet killed at this time, merely leaving a helpless newborn whom we love more than life itself! And please refrain from mentioning the word *euthanized*. It's simply not a good word to use in reference to my child."

Doyle rues the day he uttered those words because now, when the perennial topic of male cluelessness comes up, I pipe in with this story.

My point is that it's rough to leave your baby for the first time even if she's already sitting up and eating solid foods. Hopefully, by the time your baby was a few months old, you did manage to carve out some couple time for yourselves. If for some reason you've still not handed over the baby to a reliable caregiver once in a while, it's time to get a life.

There. Now that we've established the fact that you need to get a life, it's prime time to get in the good graces of a trusty baby-sitter. You may be dying to catch that movie all your girlfriends are talking about, yet hesitant to leave Junior with anyone but your parents or in-laws.

With my parents one thousand miles away and Doyle's a good hour to the west, we had no choice but to cultivate a relationship with a "date" sitter, someone we could call when an hour's drive seemed like too much hassle for one evening, but someone with whom we felt super-comfortable leaving our precious boy.

First there was Kim, a quiet seventeen-year-old who won rave reviews from other church moms. She came highly recommended, and I knew I liked her when I saw the hockey pendant around her neck. Not sure how to proceed at first, I went a little nuts buying snacks for her three hours at our house. I mean, how many chips and cookies could one thin teenager possibly eat? Since our dinner date would take place, oddly enough, during the dinner hour, I also bought her some sort of trendy deli wrap sandwiches and soda for her supper. After buying out the grocery store *and* paying her a top wage, we didn't have a whole bunch of money left to work with on our date. Good thing our out-of-town friend was buying, or we would have spent our first real (that is, without the services of freebie grandparent baby-sitting) night out at Wendy's.

Since then we've learned a thing or two about baby-sitters (ours don't eat like linebackers, number one) and nurtured strong ties with some absolutely wonderful, trustworthy baby-sitters. This gives us plenty of opportunity to keep our couple time, not to mention our social life, alive and well, and it gives Grace, Acacia, Mary Beth, and others some dough to spend at the Gap. And the kids love 'em! It's just win-win.

Now, where to find such gems?

## Ask Around

The number-one best way to find a fabulous baby-sitter is to get a personal referral from someone you trust. If Tiffany has been a boon to your friends the Joneses, taking mindful care of their munchkins and acting responsibly while at their house (that is, no boyfriends, parties, alcohol, long-distance phone calls, and so on), chances are good she'll be an asset to your clan as well. (I use the pronoun *her* just because baby-sitters are usually girls. Boys baby-sit too, obviously!)

## The 'Hood

Keep your eyes peeled for reliable-looking teenagers on your block. If you find one close by, you'll have the added bonus of proximity, which is what *close by* usually means! Then you won't have to drive far, if at all, to pick her up and drop her off.

### Your Church
Post a notice in your church bulletin saying that you are looking for a baby-sitter. If you don't know many folks, just start accosting teenagers in the foyer and asking them if they like to baby-sit.

### Your Local College Employment Office
When I was in college in Chicago, I answered several ads for baby-sitting. If you feel more comfortable with an older, more experienced baby-sitter, or if you have an affinity for a certain college or university (such as you're alumni or your church is affiliated with the college), coeds make great sitters. They also appreciate hanging out in a real house as opposed to a shoe-box dorm room. You may have to pay a little more, though.

## Smooth Bye-Byes for Baby

Use the following tips to help your baby adjust as easily as possible to your departure:

### Let Baby Get Comfortable
If you can arrange this, ask the sitter to come over and meet you and the baby before their first evening together. For your first "real" outing, ask the sitter to arrive about thirty minutes before you depart so that she and the baby can be playing together before you step out the door.

### Always Say Good-bye
Kiss and hug your baby when you leave and tell him where you're going and when you'll be back, even if you think he doesn't understand you. Don't sneak out the door—always tempting—because Baby will become much more anxious and upset if he thinks you've just vanished.

## Minimize the Histrionics

Your baby is so in tune with your moods, she can tell if you like the baby-sitter and how much. Show your enthusiasm for the sitter, and chances are Baby will catch on and think, *Gee, she's swell.* Don't cry if your baby starts crying. Bolt to the car if you have to, but a tearful episode from you sends a big, fat message that this Mommy's Night Out thing is bad, very, very bad. Don't carry on as if you're going off to fight the Crimeans instead of going to Applebee's for dessert. You'll live through this, and so will your little one. No doubt the baby-sitter will tell you Baby stopped crying before you were even out of the driveway.

## Leave Baby for Short Periods

Leave your baby with Grandpa or Aunt Stephanie or someone he knows well for fifteen-minute periods, working your way up to one hour. Your baby can then learn—without having the added angst of being with someone unfamiliar—that when you leave you'll return. Also, it's probably a good idea to start leaving Baby in someone else's good hands once in a while before separation anxiety sets in, so he already has this thing figured out.

## Relax

"A simple 'see ya later, alligator,' followed by a quick hug and a kiss can do wonders for an anxious child. Your actions show your baby that leaving is no big deal and that you'll be home again soon," the folks at www.baby center.com say.

---

Whether it's your first-ever separation or you leave your child with a caregiver daily when you go to work, leaving your baby with a baby-sitter may be wrenching. But sooner or later, you're going to have to get over your trepidation about leaving your child in someone else's care, or you'll turn into this agoraphobic weirdo who never leaves the house.

You could spend every minute with your child, but you need your own life, too—so it's wise to let her get comfortable with the fact that there are other warm, nurturing, fun people in the world who can take very good care of her. If you don't prepare her for this during her first year of life, I promise you, you won't be able to get ten feet away from your child without her having a meltdown. That doesn't mean you should run out for a night on the town three days after you bring your baby home from the hospital. But starting early, with short periods of time away, will help your baby get used to your being gone for a little while.

## The Top Ten Books for Baby's Growing Library

Dawn Faase, mother of three and bookseller at the great local children's bookstore, Pooh's Corner, jotted down her picks for Baby's top ten books. As the daughter, granddaughter, and sister of publishers (her grandpa Herman Baker founded Baker Book House in 1940), Dawn comes from a long line of absolute book zealots. She jumped at the chance to help us cull some baby-friendly gems out of the mountains of kids' books on the shelves:

1.  *Goodnight Moon, The Runaway Bunny,* and *Big Red Barn* by Margaret Wise Brown (Harper and Row). Okay, you caught me sneaking three titles under the guise of one entry. These books are classics. They are an absolute must for every child's first library. Enough said.
2.  The Dorling Kindersley Touch and Feel series (DK Publishing). This series borrows from the great idea Dorothy Kunhardt had in *Pat the Bunny* and takes it a huge step further. It covers every possible baby-favorite subject (such as toys, pets, and farm and zoo animals) and adds great photography and fun texture.
3.  *The Big Book of Beautiful Babies Board Book* by David Ellwand (Dutton). This is such a classy book. The black-and-white photo-

graphs of babies of all ethnic backgrounds are enchanting, and the rhyming text is a perfect fit. Babies love pictures of babies, and they will adore this book.

4. *Time for Bed* by Mem Fox (Harcourt). I love this book for its tender poetry and beautiful illustrations. It starts out, "It's time for bed, little mouse little mouse, darkness is falling all over the house," and it goes on with various nighttime and bedtime scenes between mothers and babies. It's the perfect winding-down book.

 **Self-Feeding Savvy**

By ten to twelve months, Baby should be able to begin to use a spoon. He probably didn't have the dexterity needed to properly hold and shove a utensil into his mouth any earlier. In the months before giving your baby a spoon, let him begin feeding himself with some soft finger foods, such as a piece of roll or bites of soft fruit, so he can get the feel of picking up food and guiding it to his mouth. But don't expect your baby to actually feed himself once you give him a spoon.

It may get pretty messy as he flips bowls of food over, dumps them on his head, and flings things from the highchair when he becomes bored. But unless you want a hunger strike on your hands, it's best to just mop up the mess and go on with your life. Don't worry. Tomato sauce won't stain your baby's hair permanently!

Self-feeding can go at a snail's pace. It can take months before a baby eats a significant amount on his own. In fact, by fifteen months only 50 percent of children spill less than half the food they attempt to get into their mouths. Be patient, though. By age two, kids will be able to do most of the feeding themselves.[2]

5. Lamaze Infant Development Book Program (Learning Curve). These books are organized and color-coded into four developmental stages. Books in the "newborn and up" category are made of chewable, suckable, smashable, surface-washable cloth. Baby, meet book. Book, meet Baby! The "nine months and up" books are in standard board book formats with colorful pictures, textures, and fabrics to add interest and fun.

 **Quotable**

"When my children were little, I read to them nightly. It's just a very cuddly time to be all wrapped up in each other. At the very heart of reading is finding the very best books, like *Goodnight Moon*. You should read in your own voice and not be too dramatic (and I'm an actor!). Remember, it's not about you; it's about them."

—John Lithgow, actor, father
of Ian, 30, Phoebe, 19, and Nathan, 18

6. *Hush, Little Baby* by Sylvia Long (Chronicle Books). This is such a neat takeoff on the well-known lullaby. Here, however, the mama is not buying the baby diamond rings and looking glasses. Instead she is showing baby hummingbirds, evening skies, crickets, and other such evening pleasures. Sylvia Long is one of my favorite illustrators.

7. *Chicka Chicka Boom Boom* by Bill Martin Jr. and John Archambault (Simon and Schuster). This book is great fun. Throughout the text, this catchy line keeps popping up: *chicka chicka BOOM boom*. If you work this right, your baby will learn quickly that when you say "chicka chicka," his or her line is "BOOM boom." They love this. This book is also a wonderful introduction to the alphabet.

8.  *Say Goodnight, Clap Hands, Tickle Tickle, All Fall Down* by
    Helen Oxenbury (Simon and Schuster). These books are just
    perfect in their simplicity. They feature all kinds of babies doing
    what babies love to do.

9.  *We're Going on a Bear Hunt* by Michael Rosen (Simon and
    Schuster). You can have a blast with this. Sit Baby down on your
    lap and rock to the rhythm of "We're going on a BEAR hunt—
    we're going to catch a BIG one—what a BEAUTIFUL day,"
    and so on. Then when you get to the river crossing, take her
    hands and SPLASH. When you get to the mud, show her
    how to SQUISH. Then SWISH through the grass, and so
    on through the story. This is guaranteed to be the beginning
    of your baby's love affair with books.

10. *Dinosaur Roar* by Paul Stickland (Dutton). I love to recommend
    this book because it is rollicking and colorful and goofy. It's a
    great introduction to colors and opposites and rhymes, and it is
    impossible to read without getting totally carried away with it!

Dear Ez,

I simply can't fathom the fact that a year has passed since Dr. Gray brought a red, caterwauling baby boy to my face to show me. I've been captivated ever since, maybe even more so now that you are such a big boy. You are still Mama's boy, and you still love to snuggle. You walk a little bowlegged and a little lopsided, like a drunk penguin. Often during the day you will return to me after a period of playtime just for a hug and a kiss, and then you're off again for more fun. You seem to need a love fix to charge up your batteries and release you to explore.

You've started eating most meals with your own ten little fingers, adeptly popping banana slices, corn Niblets, pizza crusts—whatever!—into your bottomless pit of a tummy. Sometimes when we feed you with a spoon, you get ticked off after a while, as if you want to grab that spoon and shovel food into your own mouth. Sometimes we let you, and it's not pretty! You like to examine toys and objects every which way, and you are just plain more interested in toys than your brother was at this age. Still, there's no grass growing under your feet. You are incredibly active, a regular Energizer bunny, and sometimes it's hard to keep up with you!

"Uh-oh" and "Mama" are your two first words. Playing in Jonah's room—preferably with Jonah's toys—is your favorite activity. I can tidy up all the upstairs rooms while you poke around in Jo Jo's toybox and pull his books off the shelf. You also like to pause for thirty seconds to flip the pages of a chunky board book. Pat the Bunny is a fave of yours. I can see already that life with you is never, ever going to be boring.

When Pastor Marv dedicated you to Jesus on your first birthday, he charged you to be a servant and a helper, as your name means. Your will is strong, and your heart is loving. Daddy said you would be this tough guy with a marshmallow inside someday, and I think he's right. You have brought us so much joy and love already, precious Baby Boy. We love you to pieces!

Mama

—Lorilee Craker, mother of Jonah and Ezra

# Cake, Contemplation, and Contentment

*Milemarker!* "Often, the first question at [the twelve-month visit] is about the baby's sudden new 'irritability': 'Every time we want to do anything, she gives us grief. She needs to make all the decisions. We can't....' Not all babies get independent suddenly and dramatically. But when they do, I'm always happy to see it. This is a real touchpoint if parents can see the progress it represents. Though it means the love affair of the first year is over, the burst of autonomy is normal and healthy. A baby's struggle to find her own limits will take many years. This kind of baby shows us she'll do it openly."[1]

## Where, Oh Where, Has the Time Gone?

That helpless, swaddled seven-pounder you brought home from the hospital is now a little person in her own right. She's gained weight, strength, power, and energy. She has a growing sense of self, separate and distinct from you. She knows how big she is ("Sooooo big!"), that the dog is her favorite playmate, and that sweet potatoes are yummier than squash.

Unbelievably, your sweet, compliant baby is now exhibiting all the signs of a rebellious teenager. She seems to be torn by her need to be close to you and her need to be by herself, independent. That monkey! She can be so charming one minute, showing off her budding sense of humor, and so irascible the next. Sometimes the intensity of her emotions surprises and perplexes you. It seems ludicrous, really, to ponder those first days when the thought of disciplining your baby seemed a million years away. Now she needs you to establish borders around her world. Your limits are as vital to her well-being as food and sleep.

Those first steps were an incredible sight! Captured on celluloid for all time, they marked the beginnings of her journey away from you, and thus the great paradox of motherhood: If you love her and care for her, she will—and should—leave you one day. Your fledgling will one day fly away and set up camp in a new nest, a thought steeped in both exhilaration and heartbreak.

 **Quotable**

"Yesterday when we were horsing around on the floor, my daughter Jane accidentally banged her head into my jaw. When she saw the look on my face, her blue eyes grew round and she covered my face with baby kisses. Utterly undone, I closed my eyes and tried to imprint those kisses into my memory: the softness of her skin, the lightness in her touch, the little kissing sound her lips made, the smell of pear baby shampoo and of milk breath."[2]

—Marion Winik

And now, before you can even take a deep breath and contemplate all the wondrous things that have changed in her life and yours, it falls upon you to plan a birthday celebration. While this occasion—the social event of the season in your universe—officially marks the end of the babyhood era, she will still be your baby, always and forever. But the helplessness of the beginning of her life has been left far behind on pathways of the past. New roads lead to maturity and growth. Believe it or not, your peerless baby is on her way to becoming a matchless child.

# Happy Birthday, Baby!

I am a bona fide birthday party junkie, and no bash is more fun, sweet, and wonderful than Baby's *numero uno*. I may not be a Martha disciple in many areas of domesticity, but one thing I do share with the home-arts guru is an absolute adoration of celebrating. It's time for you to plan the perfect party for your baby, a heartfelt commemoration of this life-defining year in your family's history. This means you get to start a family tradition, and that's a marvelous thing.

Traditions and keepsakes are symbols of how important your baby is to your family, and they're what help you create a family heritage. In addition, customs convey to your baby as he grows that some of the

 **"I Want You Here, But Leave Me Alone!"**

"As babies master crawling and walking between 9 and 15 months, they may go through separation anxiety. Being newly mobile gives babies a great feeling of independence. They can disappear from you at will, which they think is great fun. But once you're out of sight, they get nervous and need to know you haven't disappeared for good. Giving verbal reassurance will help them feel secure. When you hear your baby crying for you, call out that you're around. Try suggesting that she come to you (which will build her confidence as she discovers she has the power to find you). If that doesn't stop her wails, call out that you'll be there in a minute and make sure to keep the upbeat chatter going until you get there.

"Don't fake her out: If you say you're coming soon, do so. She'll catch on that you're still around even when you're out of sight, and she'll also begin to learn the idea of 'just a minute,' which will come in handy down the road. It'll also help her trust that you will keep your word—an important step for future independence."[3]

most costly possessions a family has don't come with sticker shock. The true worth of the celebration lies in the time and love necessary to create them.

Here are some ideas to make your most special cake-and-ice-cream-a-palooza a day that will live on in infamy (or at least far beyond infancy):

## Precious Scraps

Grab a couple of empty scrapbook pages and scrapbook pens and have party guests inscribe their heartfelt wishes for Baby. We did this with both our boys, and I tell you I get teary eyed every time I read what friends and family had to say to Jonah and Ezra on their first birthday.

## Write a Letter

Many of you probably already keep a journal of some sort for your baby, but what better time to pour out your hopes and dreams than on the anniversary of his birth? Save them and make a meaningful presentation to your graduate or grown-up groom someday.

## Create a Time Capsule

Didn't have time to get to the ol' time capsule when Baby was a newborn? His birthday is another perfect time. Plus now you're getting significantly more sleep and can actually do it right!

## Plant a Tree

Commemorate Baby's big day by planting a tree. Watch the two of them grow as you take your growing girl's photo beside the tree year after year.

## Make a Wish

Amy Connor of Smithtown, New York, asked the VIPs in Baby Sarah's life to contribute to a "wish box" at her first birthday. "We asked guests to put something in they'd want her to open on her 18th birthday—a poem, a prayer, a book—whatever they felt would most symbolize them and the contribution they wanted to make in her life," she told *Child* magazine. "Someone gave the sheet music to 'A Dream Is a Wish Your Heart Makes.' One friend added a book that was important to her in her early adulthood; another gave a complete set of Beatles CDs."[4]

## The Top Ten Things to Love About These Baby Days

1. The nape of Baby's neck. Mmmm!
2. The way her hair fluffs out like peach fuzz after a bath.
3. He made you and the guy you love into a family.
4. You have a valid excuse to play with rubber duckies.
5. He thinks you're the greatest singer on the planet. Aretha's got nothing on you, Mom!
6. She reduced your big, tough-guy husband to a softie who says words like, "Daddy's itty-bitty pookie poo" and "schweetie peachy pie."
7. He loves to snuggle.
8. She has very chubby thighs, and people find them absolutely charming!
9. Footie pajamas.
10. Once you became his mama, there's nothing in the world you'd rather be.

## On the Relationship Seat: How to Be a Happy Mom

Of course you're happy. You're deliriously happy, for goodness sake! After all, you wanted a baby in the worst way, and now you have one. And, yes, everyone was right when they yammered on and on about how having kids would change your entire life. Still, the peanut gallery didn't mention the baby blues or the post-breast-feeding blues for that matter. They failed to give you the 411 on how Baby's ear infections can turn Super Mom into Stupor Mom, how *reflux* means "slimy baby puke"—everywhere—and how the four walls just close in on you sometimes. But when you hear your baby's giggle—that sonic treasure!—or hold his fluffy head close to your heart, you don't regret having him, not for a minute.

You'd lasso the moon for him if you could, like Jimmy Stewart offered to do for Donna Reed in that soul-warming yuletide flick *It's a Wonderful Life*. This kid, all twenty pounds of him, could get you to lie down on train tracks for his sake or to face down a toothsome, woman-eating carnivore with a squirt gun if you had to. And if he needed a kidney, this priceless heir? They would just need to tell you where to sign up.

Your adoration for your child is immense; your commitment to his well-being, endless. Yet, if you're like many new moms, you could be a little happier, more contented, and present in the here and now, not, as actress Tracy Pollan so aptly put it, "wishing it all away." When Oprah asked Pollan for her perspective as a fourth-time mother, the forty-year-old offered a more panoramic view of motherhood. "The biggest difference I've noticed is that I'm enjoying every second of having a tiny little baby. Sam [Pollan and Michael J. Fox's firstborn] and the girls [twins Aquinnah and Schuyler] were overwhelming. I wished a lot of it away. With this baby, I'm not wishing it away at all. It's so fun."

Pollan's words hit a nerve with me. I wondered, *Am I "wishing it all away," the sleeplessness, the crabby teething days, the bruises on my legs from tripping constantly on toys, diapers, diapers, diapers?* Yes, probably I am wishing some of it away. But I strive now to notice and hold on to the fleeting beauty of the baby days, constantly reminding myself and being reminded—by mothers, related and not, on the phone, in lines, at the store—that "they grow so fast."

One way of bringing a bit of bliss to your job as a parent, then, is to consciously, intentionally seal in your mind, like a letter to yourself to be opened later, the way the nape of Baby's neck smells, the way her giggle sounds, the way her little body feels cradled in your arms. Camcorders, cameras, tape recorders, and their kin can all help you document your child's babyhood for posterity, but holding those sweet memories close is the best.

To follow are some other ways and means for reaching out to a more joyful, fulfilled, and satisfying motherhood.

### Send Guilt to the Gangplank

Guys don't get it, but for women, guilt is a given, a by-product of parenthood. I recently tried to explain to my husband that mommies fight guilt from the start: "It starts when you pee on the stick," I said. "If it's positive, you're happy, but you think, 'Should I have bought the brand-name stick?' If it's negative, you think, 'I betcha the brand-name stick would have come up positive. Why am I such a cheapo?' And on and on it goes." Guilt is just a thorough waste of time, an emotion that can drag you way down into the landfill. So you make mistakes, huh? Well, welcome to my world, not to mention the world of every new mother on the planet. Learn from your mistakes, chalk them up to experience, and move along. Next!

### Sabotage Stress

Stress not only puts your knickers (remember knickers from, like, 1980?) in a twist, but can also filter through and affect your baby's health and well-being. Even little babies can sense stress in their caregivers, and with their sense of wellness so tightly knitted to your own, this means Baby gets tense too. Experts say stress, in grownups and children alike, alters your immune response, so you're more susceptible to illness and symptoms last longer. Whenever you feel anxious or frayed, take a deep breath, a really wonderfully deep and satisfying breath. This simple act oxygenates your blood, calms you down, and rejuvenates you physically and mentally. Breathing is something you can do anytime, anywhere, and it's a great little habit to work into your day.

Some anxiety is inevitable, and a certain amount of stress can motivate you to get things done. But plenty of stress makers can be deep-sixed right now! My motto in life these days is "I can't do everything," which is to say:

I can be, most days, a good mom, an attentive partner for Doyle, and a writer, too. But I can't homeschool, garden, lead a book club, join the PTA, or for that matter come up with something brilliant for dinner night after night. Housework slides, grass grows, and the pizza man's on our speed dial, but so what? We live in a world where salad comes in a bag, prewashed and preshredded—what a marvelous innovation! You may be more like Doyle and actually find stress relief with your hands in the worm-ridden good earth, but me? Gardening is work, and I don't have time (not to mention my little bug phobia). I'm doing what I'm supposed to be doing, and the more deeply and often I make peace with that, the better.

What can slide in your life? Dishes? Buy paper plates. That candle party your cousin wants you to have for her? Just say no, unless you're quite sure you won't get uptight about who's coming and what they'll buy. Baby clutter? Drop any and all offspring at a pal's house (do the same for her later in the week), light some of those overpriced wax products, give a favorite CD a spin, and have a couple of hours of declutterizing. You'll feel like a new woman! Whatever is causing you unmerited, unnecessary stress, give it a good shove out the door and I promise you won't miss it!

Think of your stress response as a knob in your soul. When the knob gets turned up, your immunity—and Baby's—takes a hit. Your fuse shortens, and even your fat cells dig their heels in and say, "No way, José. We ain't movin'! (Debra Waterhouse, author of *Outsmarting the Female Fat Cell*, says that cortisol, a stress hormone, stimulates fat storage, especially in your tummy.) But when that knob gets turned down through exercise and other tension tamers, the opposite happens: The feel-good hormones, endorphins, flow; you resist cold bugs; and the well-being of everyone at home, including your little one, improves.

## Nurture the Nurturer

One of the very capstones of happiness as a mother is finding ways to fulfill your personal needs within the framework of your new responsibilities. My girlfriend Katie recently—and with great glee—played hooky from her wipe-a-nose workday at home. With help from her husband, her mother-in-law, and her mother, Katie grabbed a thrill-loving pal and indulged her great love for roller coasters at an amusement park six hours away. Not only did Katie get her adrenaline pumping by plummeting towards the earth at a terrifying velocity, but she and her friend stayed at a hotel overnight and enjoyed a solid twelve hours of adult conversation to and from the park. When she came home, Katie was delighted to see her babies, whom she had sincerely missed. She felt renewed and ready again to face mountains of laundry, sassy comebacks from her four-year-old, and all manner of dirty diapers and yucky noses. Yes, she's Maiya and Elise's mom, but she's also still Katie: Roller Coaster Aficionado. This year, have you somehow lost a vital part of who you are and what makes you an original? If you'll reclaim the good things that feed your soul and give you joy, *everyone* at home wins too, especially Baby.

You may not actually take off for the weekend, at least not during Baby's first year of life, but it's important to build pockets of time into your days that rejuvenate the woman inside the mom. Here's how a few seasoned mothers did just that:

### Write It Down

"I kept a journal," says writer Paula Spencer of her self-nurturing mode. "Getting all those intense new feelings down on paper became an effective method of letting off steam. New moms need outlets, ways they can mentally stretch and shake off what would otherwise miserably cramp."[5]

### Exercise

Writer Elizabeth Fishel made swimming a priority during her first, intense seasons of motherhood. "Swimming provides the decompression between my two lives, gives me that personal oasis before I return to my loved ones. And it provides a vital message to my children: that their mom takes care of herself in order to care for them," she writes. "The flickers of guilt I've occasionally felt for leaving them to take a swim are snuffed out by the knowledge that I'm able to be a better, happier, and calmer mother when I return to them. Of course, my boys are number-one in my life, and I sustain my devotion to them by taking a daily breather."[6] I absolutely love the way Fishel put that: "sustain my devotion to them." "Sustain" connotes all kinds of benefits, including nourishment, support, endurance. By swimming a few laps a day, Fishel fuels her love for her boys and gives her parenting tasks a kick-start of power and effectiveness!

## Pay Attention to Your Own Needs

Cynthia W. Sumner, in her nifty little book *Time Out for Mom…Ahhh Moments,* insists that the best caregivers are those who care for themselves: "I've…found it therapeutic to make small lifestyle changes that allow me to pay some attention to my needs each day in the midst of caring for my family."[7]

Her book is crammed with savvy tips for quickie curatives and remedials on the rush, like a ten-minute home facial, a half-hour at the library—by yourself—before grocery shopping, and the art of self-massage. Currently, one of my favorite television shows is *Trading Spaces,* the quirky cable gem in which neighbors swap houses for a weekend of redecorating. If I time things just right, and usually this does work, Ezra is down for a nap and Jonah takes his hour-long "quiet time," which means I can sit down with a steaming cup of something heavenly and vegetate as Hildie or Vern or one of the other designers works their magic. During the commercials, I speed clean by loading the dishwasher or picking up toys. Depending on the state of my mental health, I may skip the housework and flip through a glossy catalog or magazine.

-------

There are myriad ways to create and reclaim the strength, patience, and positive attitude to meet all those twenty-four-hour-a-day mom duties, to truly balance your life for maximum joy and contentedness. Throughout these pages I have tried to give you my best ideas for nurturing your spirit through this very special, if stressful, season in your family's life:

- Falling in love with that guy you made the baby with—remember him?—all over again (see page 89).

- Finding and keeping good, true pals who make your life easier, more fun, and rich with meaning and connectedness (see page 98).

- Dwelling in a place of love and wisdom by remaining close to your Father's heart (see page 144).

Motherhood is not all it's cracked up to be—it's more. Make the most of this precious year with your baby. If the sisterhood of mothers, past and present, is to be trusted, you will surely look back on this year as one of the most prized seasons of your life.

# Notes

## Feed Me First!

1. Sally Tusa, "Breast or Bottle?" *Baby Talk,* September 2001, 38-43.
2. Janet Tamaro, *So That's What They're For: Breastfeeding Basics* (Holbrook, Mass.: Adams Media, 1998), 91.
3. LaLecheLeague.com, 2002.
4. Ruth A. Lawrence, M.D., and Robert M. Lawrence, M.D., *Breastfeeding: A Guide for the Medical Profession, Fifth Edition* (St. Louis: Mosby, 1980), 369.
5. Breastfeedingbasics.com, 2002.
6. Gwen Zepeda, "Breastfeeding," Hipmama.com, 2002.

## Month One

1. T. Berry Brazelton, M.D., *Touchpoints: The Essential Reference: Your Child's Emotional and Behavioral Development* (New York: Perseus, 1992), 55.
2. "First Year Q and A," *Child,* October 2001, 56.
3. Amy Einhorn, *The Fourth Trimester: Advice, Humor, and Inspiration for New Moms on Surviving the First Six Weeks and Beyond* (New York: Crown, 2001), 33.

## Month Two

1. Marie Osmond, *Behind the Smile,* as quoted by *Good Housekeeping,* May 2001, 98.
2. Depressionafterdelivery.com, 2002.
3. Stacy Colino, "The Silent Epidemic," *Child,* April 2002, 48.
4. Colino, "Epidemic," 48.
5. Dr. Alan Greene, M.D., FAAP, "The Scoop on Colic," AmericanBaby.com, May 2002.

## Month Three

1. Nell Bernstein, "Desperately Seeking Sleep," *Baby Talk,* February 2000, 39.

2. "Sleep Deprivation As Bad As Alcoholic Impairment, Study Suggests," CNN.com, 2000.

3. Trisha Thompson, "Reality Check," *Parenting,* April 2002, 153.

## Month Four

1. Paul Reiser, *Babyhood* (New York: Avon, 1997), 141.

2. Jodi Mindell, *Getting Your Baby to Sleep,* as quoted by Linda Henry, "Goodnight Baby," *Parenting,* April 2002, 122.

3. Mindell, as quoted by Henry, "Goodnight," 122.

4. Mindell, as quoted by Henry, "Goodnight," 122.

5. "Babybytes," *Child,* May 2002, 53.

## Month Five

1. Anita Sethi, "Baby Steps," *Baby Talk,* September 2001, 27-8.

2. Dr. William Sears, "Top 7 Illnesses," *Baby Talk,* October 2001, 30-1.

3. Arlene Eisenberg, Heidi E. Murkoff, and Sandee E. Hathaway, B.S.N, *What to Expect the First Year* (New York: Workman, 1996), 586.

4. Pamela Satran, "The BT List: Top Ten Pregnancy Fantasies," *Baby Talk,* May 2001, 72.

5. Debra Waterhouse, *Outsmarting the Female Fat Cell—After Pregnancy* (New York: Hyperion, 2002), 139.

## Month Six

1. Paula Spencer, "Friends," *Child,* May 2002.

2. Spencer, "Friends."

3. Camerin Courtney, "What Single Women Wish You Knew," *Today's Christian Woman,* May 2002, 51.

4. Courtney, "Single Women," 51.

5. Spencer, "Friends."

6. Vicki Iovine, "Girlfriend to Girlfriend," *Child,* May 2001, 105.

7. "Ear Infections," BabyCenter.com, 2002.

## Month Seven

1. "Developmental Milestones: Your Seven-Month-Old," BabyCenter.com, 2002.

2. Debra Waterhouse, *Outsmarting the Female Fat Cell—After Pregnancy* (New York: Hyperion, 2002), 33.

3. Waterhouse, *Outsmarting,* 33.

4. Waterhouse, *Outsmarting,* 33.

5. Waterhouse, *Outsmarting,* 33.

6. Waterhouse, *Outsmarting,* 33.

7. Waterhouse, *Outsmarting,* 33.

8. Jack Moore, *97 Ways to Make a Baby Laugh* (New York: Workman, 1997).

9. Moore, *97 Ways.*

## Month Eight

1. Elaine Floyd, C.F.P., "Family Ties/Money Talk," *Fit Pregnancy,* April/May 2002, 46.

2. Heather Harpham Kopp, *Praying the Bible for Your Baby* (Colorado Springs: Water-Brook, 1998), 3.

## Month Nine

1. Brazelton, *Touchpoints,* 120.

2. "Your Nine-Month-Old's Development," BabyCenter.com, 2002.

3. Edward R. Christophersen, Ph.D, "Disciplining Your Baby," BabyCenter.com, 2002.

4. Deborah Geigis Berry, "Traveling with Baby," *Baby Talk,* February 2002, 45.

## Month Ten

1. "10 Months: Fun and Games," *American Baby's First Year of Life* (special issue published by *American Baby*), 69.

2. Foreword by Dr. James Dobson, *Complete Book of Baby and Child Care* (Colorado Springs: Focus on the Family, 1997), 226.

3. Paula Spencer, "Positive Parenting," *Baby Talk,* August 2001, 32.

4. Stephanie Wood, *Baby Talk Magazine's First Year Guide,* 2000, 24.

## Month Eleven

1. "Separation Anxiety," BabyCenter.com, 2002.

2. Barbara Durkin, "First Year Q and A," *Child,* February 2002, 36.

## Month Twelve

1. Brazelton, *Touchpoints,* 134-5.

2. Marion Winik, "Baby Love," *Child,* May 2002, 110.

3. Mary Rose Almasi, "Independence Angst," *Child,* October 2001, 56.

4. Jessica Brown, "First Birthday," *Child,* June/July 2002, 69.

5. Paula Spencer, "Six Secrets of a Happy Mom," *Parenting,* April 2002, 99.

6. Elizabeth Fishel, "Time for Myself," *Child,* May 2002, 148.

7. Cynthia W. Sumner: *Time Out for Moms: Ahhh Moments* (Grand Rapids: Zondervan, 2000).